Essential
Provence
&
The Côte d'Azur

by Teresa Fisher

Teresa Fisher is a confirmed Francophile and
experienced travel writer who has written or
contributed to numerous guides on holiday
destinations throughout Europe including the AA
publications *Village France, Hotels and B&B in
France, CityPack Munich* and *CityPack
Amsterdam.*

AA Publishing

Above: *The pace of life in Provence is relaxed*

Page 1: *Rooftops of the hill village Le Barroux*

Page 5a: *Commercial lavender growing*
5b: *Changing the guard in Monaco*

Page15a: *The Calanques near Cassis*
15b: *Giacometti sculpture at the Fondation Maecht*

Page 27a: *Aups is an attractive agricultural town*
27b: *Alpes road marker*

Page 91a: *Figurines called* santons *for sale*
91b: *Cannes Film Festival sculpture*

Page 117a: *Mardi Gras time in Nice*
117b: *Pastis from Marseille*

Find out more about AA Publishing and the wide range of services the AA provides by visiting our Web site at www.theaa.co.uk.

Written by Teresa Fisher

Edited, designed and produced by AA Publishing.
© The Automobile Association 1998
Maps © The Automobile Association 1998
Reprinted Nov 1998; Jun 1999; Feb 2000

Distributed in the United Kingdom by AA Publishing, Norfolk House, Priestley Road, Basingstoke, Hampshire, RG24 9NY.

A CIP catalogue record for this book is available from the British Library.

ISBN 0 7495 1620 8

The Automobile Association retains the copyright in the original edition © 1998 and in all subsequent editions, reprints and amendments.

All rights reserved. No part of this publication may be reproduced, stored in a retrieval system, or transmitted in any form or by any means – electronic, photocopying, recording or otherwise – unless the written permission of the publishers has been obtained beforehand. This book may not be sold, resold, hired out or otherwise disposed of by way of trade in any form of binding or cover other than that in which it is published, without the prior consent of the publisher.

The contents of this publication are believed correct at the time of printing. Nevertheless, the publishers cannot be held responsible for any errors or omissions or for changes in the details given in this guide or for the consequences of any reliance on the information provided by the same. Assessments of attractions, hotels, restaurants and so forth are based upon the author's own experience and, therefore, descriptions given in this guide necessarily contain an element of subjective opinion which may not reflect the publisher's opinion or dictate a reader's own experience on another occasion.

We have tried to ensure accuracy in this guide, but things do change and we would be grateful if readers would advise us of any inaccuracies they may encounter.

Published by AA Publishing, a trading name of Automobile Association Developments Limited, whose registered office is Norfolk House, Priestley Road, Basingstoke, Hampshire, RG24 9NY. Registered number 1878835.

Colour separation: BTB, Digital Imaging, Whitchurch, Hampshire

Printed and bound in Italy by Printer Trento srl

Contents

About this Book

KEY TO SYMBOLS

✚ map reference to the maps found in the What to See section (see below)

✉ address or location

☎ telephone number

◷ opening times

🍴 restaurant or café on premises or near by

Ⓜ nearest underground train station

🚍 nearest bus/tram route

🚆 nearest overground train station

🛳 ferry crossings and excursions by boat

✈ travel by air

ℹ tourist information

♿ facilities for visitors with disabilities

✋ admission charge

↔ other places of interest near by

❓ other practical information

▶ indicates the page where you will find a fuller description

Essential *Provence & The Côte d'Azur* is divided into five sections to cover the most important aspects of your visit to Provence.

Viewing Provence pages 5–14
An introduction to Provence & The Côte d'Azur by the author.

    Features of Provence & The Côte d'Azur
    Essence of Provence & The Côte d'Azur
    The Shaping of Provence & The Côte d'Azur
    Peace and Quiet
    Famous of Provence & The Côte d'Azur

Top Ten pages 15–26
The author's choice of the Top Ten places to visit in Provence & The Côte d'Azur, each with practical information.

What to See pages 27–90
The four main areas of Provence & The Côte d'Azur, each with its own brief introduction and an alphabetical listing of the main attractions within the area.

    Practical information
    Snippets of 'Did You Know…' information
    3 suggested walks
    2 suggested tours
    2 features

Where To... pages 91–116
Detailed listings of the best places to eat, stay, shop, take the children and be entertained.

Practical Matters pages 117–24
A highly visual section containing essential travel information.

Maps

All map references are to the individual maps found in the What to See section of this guide.

For example, St Tropez has the reference ✚ 69C1 – indicating the page on which the map is located and the grid square in which St Tropez is to be found. The maps used can be found in the index.

Prices

Where appropriate, an indication of the cost of an establishment is given by **£** signs: **£££** denotes higher prices, **££** denotes average prices, while **£** denotes lower charges.

Star Ratings

Most of the places described in this book have been given a separate rating:

✪✪✪   Do not miss
✪✪   Highly recommended
✪   Worth seeing

Viewing
Provence

Teresa Fisher's Provence & The Côte d'Azur

It looked astonishingly beautiful in Maurice Pagnol's films *Jean de Florette* and *Manon des Source*, and Peter Mayle's best-selling books present life there as an idyll, but what is Provence really like?

Is it the untamed marshes of the Camargue; or the snow-clad mountains of the Alps; or perhaps the shimmering heat of the beautiful beaches and the exotic palms of the chic resorts which line the Mediterranean coastline?

Most visitors are at a loss to know where to start, such is the variety of the landscape and the wealth of ancient history, but for many the true essence of Provence can be found in the myriad sleepy medieval villages, precariously perched on steep hillsides or hidden in a sun-drenched landscape of silvery olive groves, vineyards and parasol pines, splashed with poppy fields and scented stripes of lavender, stretching like mauve corduroy across the countryside, the air heavy with all the perfumes of Provence, the countryside painted with the vivid palette of Van Gogh and Cézanne.

No wonder Provence and the Côte d'Azur is France's most visited region, with its exceptional cultural heritage, and its rich diversity of landscape, cuisine, climate and peoples. Yet despite its popularity, it is still possible to escape the tourist hordes and discover your own hidden delights – tiny sun-kissed vineyards and secret sun-baked coves; bustling markets; romantic *châteaux* or a dusty game of *boules*; coffee and croissants in a village café, *pastis* in the bar...

New visitors soon fall under the region's spell. Those who already know it remain enchanted, returning year after year for a taste of *la vie Provençale*.

Defining the Boundaries
The regions of Provence and the Côte d'Azur are difficult to define as, since the Roman *Provincia* of 125 BC, Provence's borders have moved countless times. Today it comprises the region Provence-Alpes-Côte d'Azur, made up of the *départements*: Alpes-Maritimes, Bouches-du-Rhône, Alpes-de-Haute Provence, Hautes-Alpes, Var and Vaucluse. Officially the Côte d'Azur stretches from the French-Italian frontier to St Raphaël, although the expression is frequently applied to the whole French Riviera as far as Marseille.

Features of Provence & The Côte d'Azur

Geography
- One of 22 regions of France
- *Départements*: Alpes-Maritimes, Alpes-de-Haute-Provence, Bouches du Rhône, Hautes Alpes, Vaucluse and Var.
- Surface area: 31,436sq km (Monaco: 2sq km)
- Protected monuments and buildings: 1,500
- Highest mountain: La Meije (3,983m)

People
- Inhabitants: 4.5 million (including 375,000 foreigners) 90% live in large cities and their suburbs.
- People with second homes here: 400,000
- Largest city: Marseille (population: 1.2 million)
- Annual visitors to coast: 8 million
- Tourist revenue: F40 billion

Climate
- Average annual temperature range: -1°C–22°C (mountains); 6°C–24°C (coast)
- Sea temperature range: 10°–25°C
- Annual hours of sunshine: 3,000 (over 300 days a year)
- Annual rainfall: 55–82cm (Nov and Mar are wettest)
- Mistral wind: up to 290km/h; 100–150 days a year

Agriculture & Industry
- Percentage of France's total production: lemons (70%); cut flowers (50%), fruit and vegetables (20%); rice (25%); melons (30%); olives (52%); grapes (50%)
- Flowers produced: 172 million roses; 188 million carnations
- Percentage of world production: lavender oil (70%)
- Farmers: 20,000
- 1,500 fishermen catch 20,000 tons (including 10,000 tons of sardines!)

Wine
- Classified wine regions: 17
- *Appellation d'Origine Contrôlée* (AOC) wines: 16
- Vineyards: 16 per cent of region's agricultural land; 11 per cent of France's vineyards
- Average size of vineyard: 6 hectares
- People employed by the wine trade: 20,000

Economy
Provence and the Côte d'Azur is vital to France's economy, mainly due to Marseille, the country's second city and one of the world's leading ports. 90 per cent of Marseille's imports is oil and the massive surrounding industrial area produces 85 per cent of France's aluminium and 30 per cent of its natural gas. Tourism plays a major role, along with research and high-tech industries, notably the Nice-Sophia-Antipolis technological park, France's 'silicon valley'.

Facing page: *A taste of Provence – cobbled stones, golden sunlight and sleepy mountaintop villages*

Below: *A market trader sells his burnished sweet chestnuts*

Essence of Provence & The Côte d'Azur

The many facets and charms of Provence and the Côte d'Azur are impossible to chart, so many and varied are they, making the choice almost impossible. Should you pack your paintbox, walking boots, swimsuit, skis or all of them? One suggestion is that on your first visit, concentrate solely on the ambiance – the brilliant sunshine, the sparkling air, the superb food, the unforgettable scenery and the friendly locals – for it is certain you will become a devotee and return again and again to experience what the addicted already know but would rather keep to themselves!

Street artists in Avignon capture the essence of Provence on canvas

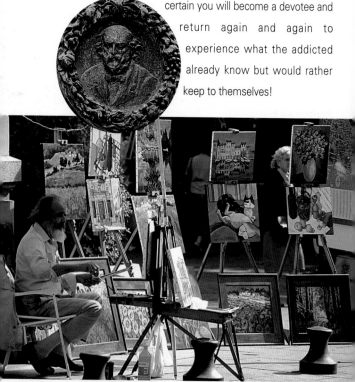

THE **10** ESSENTIALS

If you only have a short time to visit Provence, or would like to get a really complete picture of the region, here are the essentials:

Relax by the waterfront or on a shady terrace

• **Soak up the sun on one of the Riviera's sandy beaches**, or relax under the shade of a classic striped parasol.

• **Visit a perfumery in Grasse**, and create your very own Provençal scent (➤ 88).

• **Taste some of the world's finest wines** at Châteauneuf-du-Pape.

• **Taste *la vraie bouillabaisse*** in Marseille, near the old port where the dish originated.

• **Spot the rich and famous at the Cannes Film Festival**, the glitziest, most glamorous event of them all.

• **Try your hand at gambling** in Monte Carlo's world-famous casino.

• **Don your diamonds and the latest in *haute couture* design**, and promenade the waterfront at St Tropez, admiring its ostentatious yachts and gin palaces.

• **Splash through the marshes of the Camargue** on horseback, accompanied by local *gardian* cowboys.

• **Go shopping in a bright, bustling village market**, and treat yourself to a relaxing picnic of goodies –

goats' cheese, tomatoes, olives and wine – in the sleepy surrounding countryside.

• **Join locals in a game of *boules*** – this ancient game originated here and, although it is now played all round the world, the most fiercely-contested games still take place in the shady squares of Provence.

The mountain village of Gourdon has an amazing view of the River Loup

9

The Shaping of Provence & The Côte d'Azur

c900,000 BC
First signs of human settlement.

c3,500 BC
First *borie* villages (➤ 19).

c600 BC
Greeks found port of Massalia (Marseille) and introduce olives, vines and ceramics.

300 BC
Celtic invasions of Provence.

218 BC
Hannibal crosses region to reach Italy.

125 BC
Romans conquer southern Gaul and name it *Provincia*.

58–52 BC
Caesar's conquest of Gaul.

3rd–5th Century AD
Spread of Christianity.

395
Arles becomes administrative capital of Roman Gaul.

476
Fall of Roman Empire.

536
Provence comes under Frankish rule.

8–10th Century
Saracens invade southern France; Provence becomes part of the Carolingian Empire.

855
Kingdom of Provence created for Charlemagne's grandson, Charles the Bald.

1032
Provence becomes part of Holy Roman Empire.

12–14th Century
Troubadour poetry and 'Courtly Love' flourishes (➤ 47).

1266
Charles I of Anjou, (already Duke of Provence) is crowned King of Provence.

1308
The Genoese Grimaldi family purchase the estate of Monaco.

1309
Frenchman, Clement V, becomes Pope; Papacy established in Avignon until 1376.

1409
Aix University is founded.

1481
Death of Good King René, last count of Provence (➤ 52). Region falls to France.

1501
Provençal Parliament founded in Aix.

1535
Nostradamus born at St-Rémy.

1539
French replaces Provençal, the *Langue d'Oc*, as official language.

1559
Town and duchy of Orange fall to William of Nassau, Prince of Orange.

1691
Nice occupied by the French, but returned to Savoy in 1696.

1720
Great Plague kills over 100,000 people.

1789
French Revolution, Republicans adopt army song 'La Marseillaise' (➤ 55).

1791
France annexes Avignon and the Comtat Venaissin.

1814
Napoléon lands in Provence.

1830
Provençal poet laureate Frédéric Mistral is born at Maillane.

1830s
Beginnings of tourism on the French Riviera.

1839
Artist Paul Cézanne born

10

at Aix-en-Provence.

1854
Foundation of the Félibrige literary circle with the aim of promoting the Provençal language.

1855
Paris and Avignon linked by rail.

1860
Nice votes to join France.

1866
Monte-Carlo founded; Casino opened in 1878.

1888
Van Gogh moves to Arles from Paris.

1920s–30s
Côte d'Azur becomes a fashionable summer resort.

1928
Camargue National Park created.

1933
Waters of the Rhône first harnessed for energy.

1942
Nazis invade southern France.

1944
Allied troops land on the Côte d'Azur.

1946
Picasso moves to Antibes.

1947
First Cannes Film Festival.

1956
Monaco's Prince Rainer III marries Grace Kelly.

1959
Floods in Fréjus kill 421.

1962
Nice–Côte d'Azur airport opened.

1962
Algerian war of independence; Many French North Africans (*pieds-noirs*) settle in Provence.

1968
Marseille

harbour becomes too small for rapid industrial growth; Etang de Berre industrial harbour opened.

1970
Autoroute du Soleil completed.

1972
Regionalisation of French *départements*; five combined to create the region 'Provence–Âlpes–Côte d'Azur'.

1981
Paris and Marseille linked by TGV.

1980s
Extreme right political parties gain popularity in key Provençal cities.

1992
Freak floods devastate parts of the Vaucluse and claim lives in Vaison-la-Romaine.

Monte Carlo's heyday

11

Peace & Quiet

Nature has been infinitely generous with Provence and the Côte d'Azur. You only need to wander through the fields and forests, to hike in the hills, gorges and mountains or to stroll along the shoreline to discover a vast array of flora and fauna in its varied habitats. It is, without doubt, a naturalist's paradise.

The Coast

With the colourful birdlife of the Riviera coast, in particular the bright yellow serins and Sardinian warblers of the rocky Esterel coast, it is easy to forget that hidden out of sight, the Mediterranean supports an abundance of marine creatures. Port Cros, one of Hyères' Îles d'Or, and France's only offshore national park, provides a rare opportunity to see the region's rich underwater life. Armed with a mask and flippers, and following a unique underwater path, it is possible to swim with vividly-coloured fish (sea peacocks, black-faced blennies), while octopuses and jellyfish lurk among beds of Neptune grass, sponges and sea anemones.

Eagle owls and flamingos – just two of the wonders of the Camargue

Provence's best-known wildlife location and one of Europe's most important wetlands, is the Camargue, famous for its white horses, black bulls, pink flamingos and some of Europe's most exotic birds (► 17).

The Hinterland

In the *arrière pays*, north-west of the Camargue, lies a rarely-visited area – the Plaine de la Crau, a stony plain with sun-bleached scrub and the occasional

rockpool, ideal habitat for both insects and reptiles. Indeed, five species of non-poisonous snake can be found here, including the rare Montpellier snake. Look out also for pin-tailed sandgrouse, cream-bibbed pratincole and the dazzling orange, yellow, green, blue and black bee-eater, one of Provence's most colourful birds, which feeds on bees and dragonflies, caught on the wing. The low, craggy limestone Alpilles *massif* beyond attracts birds of prey including Bonelli's eagle, Egyptian vultures and eagle owls, while its rich *garrigue* vegetation harbours warblers, hoopoes and blue rock thrushes.

One of Provence's special delights is to ramble through the region's extensive brushwood habitats (locally called *garrigue*), where the air is fragrant with lavender and wild herbs – rosemary, thyme, basil, marjoram and tarragon – the delicious *Herbes de Provence* so prominent in regional cuisine.

The area's sunshine and favourable climate allow many interesting trees to grow, with olive and oak predominant in lower regions, pines, almonds and neat rows of cypresses on the hillsides of the interior, and an abundance of fruit trees. After all, Provence is the market garden of France.

The Mountains

Up in the Hautes Alpes, the Parc Régional de Queyras is a wild, forgotten corner of the alps bordering Italy, renowned for its rare wild flowers. To the south, one of France's most beautiful alpine reserves – the Mercantour National Park – provides sanctuary for most of Europe's mountain animal species, including wild boar, marmot, chamois, ibex, mouflon (wild sheep) as well as bright butterflies and myriad alpine flowers. Their sweet, heady perfume attracts a busy insect life of beetles, bugs and bees – an endless supply of food for the 18 types of bat common to the area.

The snow-capped peaks of the Provençal Alps are never far away

La Pêche

Provence is a paradise for fishermen, with trout, salmon and eel in abundance in the region's countless rivers and lakes. Sea-fishing is also popular with well-organised trips from most ports (▶ 115). Look out for a method of fishing unique to the sandy rivers of the Camargue - *pêche à pied* (lit. 'fishing by foot') - where tiny molluscs called *tellines* are gathered by hand, served locally with garlic and parsley as a delicious regional *hors d'oeuvre* (▶ 36 and 95).

13

Famous of Provence & The Côte d'Azur

Ever since Dijonais vineyard owner, Stephen Liegeard visited the Mediterranean in 1887, and exclaimed 'Côte d'Azur!' (thereby christening an already popular winter health resort), a rich assortment of actors, artists, writers and royalty have been attracted to this southern coast of France, from Queen Victoria to Pablo Picasso, and from Frédéric Mistral to Peter Mayle, all seduced by the beauty of its landscapes and the sparkling azure sea. As Nietsche wrote in 1883: 'Here, the days follow on with a beauty that I would describe as almost insolent. I have never lived through a winter of such constant perfection'.

Star Quality

It was not until the 1930s that the Riviera became a summer resort, made fashionable by visiting Americans including Harpo Marx, Isadora Duncan, who met her tragic death here when her scarf became entangled round the axle of her open car, and writer, F Scott Fitzgerald. Nowadays the Riviera remains home to Brigitte Bardot, Joan Collins, Johnny Halliday, Roger Moore and a whole host of celebrities.

Inspirational Provence

Many writers have been drawn to Provence over the years, and it has been the focus of countless literary masterpieces (see panel). However, it is the artists who have left the deepest imprint on the region – Renoir, Dufy, Matisse, Cézanne and Van Gogh to name but a few. They have immortalised Provence's most prestigious sites on canvas, hypnotised by the rich palette of landscapes and the almost magical, incandescent light which has provided inspiration over the centuries – as it still does today for a new generation of artists and writers.

Prince Rainier of Monaco with the late Princess Grace

Top Ten

1
The Calanques

+ 28B1

ℹ Cassis Tourist Office: place Baragnon (☎ 04 42 01 71 17)

♿ None

✋ Expensive

↔ Cassis (▶ 57), Marseille (▶ 54)

? One-hour visits by boat with commentary from 9–6 daily

The most dramatic scenery of the French Riviera – dazzling white cliffs plunging into the sparkling turquoise waters of magnificent mini-fjords.

This fjord-like landscape is unique in Europe. Just outside Cassis, the coast is broken up by a series of tiny, narrow creeks or *calanques*, lying at the foot of sheer limestone cliffs. The vertical, sun-scorched rock faces are popular with climbers and the clear, deep water is ideal for bathing, making the area a popular weekend retreat for the nearby Marseillais.

The Calanques can only be reached by pleasure cruiser from Cassis or on foot, following a clearly-signed path across the heather and gorse of the high cliff tops, with a steep scramble down to the beaches. The first and longest *calanque*, Port Miou, is one of the most picturesque, lined

A stunning view across azure sea to the white, sun-bleached rocks of the Calanques

with yachts and pleasure craft. Calanque Port-Pin is the smallest, with a tiny shingle beach shaded by pines (hence the name, although many trees here were destroyed by a massive forest fire in 1990). En Vau, the third inlet, is the most spectacular, with stark precipitous cliffs and needle-like rocks rising from the sea. The 1½-hour walk to reach it, and the ensuing steep descent to the sandy beach keeps it free from crowds.

Further west, the Sormiou and Morgiou creeks can be reached by car. In 1991, French diver Henri Cosquer discovered a Stone-Age underwater grotto deep below sea level at Sormiou. It is decorated with ancient paintings of prehistoric animals, similar to those found at Lascaux in the Dordogne. There are doubts about the paintings' authenticity, but, unfortunately, no palaeolithic experts have the ability to dive to 32m in order to decide whether they are genuine.

2
The Camargue

A strangely melancholic marshland, renowned for its passionate people, its traditions, its silver-cream horses, black bulls and salmon-pink flamingos.

No area in France matches the Camargue for its landscape: brackish lagoons, flat rice fields and salty marshes, sand spits and coastal dunes, tufted with coarse, spiky grass and interlaced with shallow streams and canals. Even its boundaries – the lesser and greater Rhône deltas and the sea – are forever-shifting. This extraordinary landscape harbours an outstanding variety of wildlife, and the unique lifestyle of the Camarguais cowboys.

The people of the Camargue are hardy folk. They live in low, thatched, white-washed cottages with bulls horns over the door to ward off evil spirits. They proudly guard the Camarguais heritage, by wearing traditional costume and raising horses and cattle on ranches, or *manades*. Contrary to popular belief, the famous white horses are not wild. They are actually owned by a *manadier* or breeder, but are left to roam semi-free. Some are also used for trekking expeditions. The small, black local bulls with their distinctive lyre-shaped horns, are bred for the ring (▶ 50). Watching a mounted *gardian* drive his herd through the marshes is a truly unforgettable sight!

The Camargue also offers sanctuary to some of Europe's most exotic water birds including purple herons and stone curlews. It is the only place in Europe where flamingoes breed regularly and in their greatest numbers between April and September. The best months for bird watching are from April to June and from September to February.

✚ 28A1

Parc Ornithologique du Pont-du-Gau (Bird Sanctuary)

✉ Pont-de-Gau/DN570

☎ 04 90 97 82 62

🕐 Feb–Nov, daily 9–sunset

♿ Few

🎫 Free

Manade Jacques Bon, Camargue

✉ Le Mas de Peint, 13200 Le Sambuc

☎ 04 90 97 20 62

❓ Professional ranch with rodeos and tours on horseback

Musée Camarguais

✉ Mas du Pont de Rousty

☎ 04 90 97 10 82

🕐 Apr–Sep, 9:15–6:45; Oct–Mar, 10–4:15 except Tue. Closed 1 Jan, 1 May, 25 Dec

♿ Good

🎫 Moderate

Silver-cream horses – one of the classic sights of the Camargue

17

3

Fondation Maeght, St-Paul-de-Vence

A world in which modern art can both find its place and that otherworldliness which used to be called supernatural.

85A3

06570 Saint Paul

04 93 32 09 79

Oct–Jun, 10–12:30, 2:30–6; Jul–Sep, 10–7

Café

Few

Very expensive

St Paul-de-Vence (► 89), Vence (► 90), Cagnes (► 84)

Cinema and art library

These words were spoken by André Malraux, Minister of Cultural Affairs, during the inaugural speech of Foundation Maeght in 1964, a beautiful gallery which has since become one of the most distinguished modern art museums in the world. It was the brainchild of Aimé and Marguerite Maeght, who were art dealers and close friends of Matisse, Miró, Braque, Bonnard and Chagall, and it was their private collection that formed the basis of the museum. Their aim was to create the ideal environment in which to display contemporary art, and to achieve this they worked in close collaboration with the Catalan architect, José-Luis Sert.

The small artful gallery which resulted is hidden amidst umbrella pines above the quaint hilltop village of St Paul-

de-Vence. It is surrounded by a small park which contains a collection of sculptures, mosaics and murals. The building itself blends into its natural surroundings, with massive windows, light traps in the roof, and extraordinary white cylindrical 'sails' atop the building. These are not solely decorative, but serve the dual purpose of collecting rainwater to work the fountains.

The Fondation Maeght's remarkable permanent collection is comprised entirely of 20th-century art and includes works by nearly

The Fondation's garden is a veritable forest of sculptures

every major artist of the past 50 years. These are shown in rotation throughout the year, except during summer when temporary exhibitions are held. The star sights include the Cour Giacometti – a tiled courtyard peopled with skinny Giacometti figures – Chagall's vast, joyful canvas – *La Vie*, and Miró's *Labyrinthe* – a fantastic multi-level maze of fountains, trees, mosaics and sculptures. There is also a chapel in the grounds, which contains stained glass by Braque, Ubec and Marq. It was built in memory of the Maeght's son who died in 1953 at the age of 11. The bookshop and cinema are also worth visiting.

4
Gordes &
the Abbeye de Sénanque

Famous for its artists' colony, magnificent Cistercian abbey and ancient Borie village, Gordes makes an ideal centre for touring the Lubéron.

Gordes is justifiably rated one of the most beautiful villages in France. Its grandiose church and Renaissance feudal château, rise from a golden plinth on a spur of Mont Ventoux, surrounded by narrow cobbled streets and tiers of golden sandstone houses which spill down the steep, stony slopes. During World War II, many buildings were ruined or abandoned and the village fell into decline until the 1960s, when Cubist André l'Hote, Constructivist Victor Vasarély and other artists brought new life to the village, restoring the delightful Renaissance houses and setting up attractive galleries, studios and boutiques. The castle is now Vasarély's home. Its museum contains over 1,000 of his vivid abstract paintings and dazzling geometric designs.

In a secluded valley nearby, bathed in a sea of lavender, is one of the great symbols of Provence – the sun-bleached Cistercian abbey of Sénanque is one of France's purest remaining vestiges of 12th-century religious architecture. The monks still follow a secret medieval recipe to cococt a pungent, herb-flavoured yellow liqueur called Sénancole.

Just south of Gordes, the most famous collection of *bories* in France lie hidden in dusty scrubland. These extraordinary beehive-shaped, dry-stone huts sheltered the earliest farmers and semi-nomadic shepherds as early as the 3rd century BC. This particular village was inhabited as recently as the last century, and is the largest and most complete of its kind in the world.

39B2

Gordes Tourist Office: Le Château (☎ 04 90 72 02 75)

Fontaine-de-Vaucluse (► 41), Roussillon (► 24)

Château de Gordes

☎ 04 90 72 02 89

Jul–Aug, daily 10–12, 2–6; Sep–Jun, Wed–Mon 10–12, 2–5. Closed 1 May, 25 Dec

Moderate

Roussillon (► 24); Fontaine-de-Vaucluse (► 41); villages of the Lubéron (► 40, 41 & 43).

Villages des Bories

route de Cavaillon

☎ 04 90 72 03 48

Daily 9–sunset.

Good

Moderate

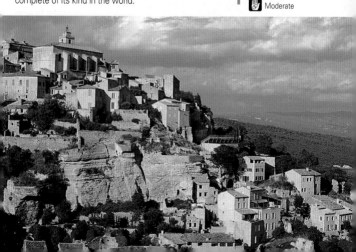

5
Grand Canyon du Verdon

✚ 69B3

✉ Verdon Accueil, Aiguines

☎ 04 94 70 21 64

↔ Aups (▶ 68); Gréoux-les-Bains (▶ 73); Moustiers-Ste-Marie (▶ 74).

❓ Useful contacts: Bureau des Guides (☎ 04 92 77 30 50) for walkers and climbers; Ranch Les Pioneers (☎ 04 92 77 38 30) for horse-riding; Verdon Insolite (☎ 04 77 33 57) for canoeing, rafting and mountain-biking; Verdon Passion (☎ 04 92 74 69 77) for hang-gliding and bi-planes.

The Canyon boasts some of the most spectacular scenery in Provence

The deepest, longest, wildest canyon in Europe is like a dream-come-true for canoeists, climbers, white-water rafters and other sports lovers.

Over the centuries the Verdon river, a tributary of the mighty Durance, has scored a magnificent gorge in the limestone plateau of the Alpes-de-Haute-Provence, stretching a staggering 21km from the Pont de Soleils down to the vast man-made lake of Sainte-Croix. In places it is over 800m deep, the second deepest gorge in the world after the Grand Canyon and one of the great natural wonders of Provence. It was first explored as late as 1905 by Isadore Blanc. Before that people were deterred by local stories of devils and 'wild men'.

The canyon is best approached from Castellane to the east. The bed of the canyon is impassable, and the river is only negotiable by trained sportsmen or with an official guide. Instead, spectacular winding roads hairpin along the clifftops on both sides of the gorge, with frequent *belvédères* to park the car and peer giddily down to the green waters of the Verdon.

Drivers face a difficult decision whether to follow the northern '*Route des Crêtes*', with its many magnificent viewpoints, or the southern '*Corniche Sublime*', through the ancient hilltop villages of Trigance and Aiguines. Hardened walkers usually opt for the latter, leaving the road at the Pont Sublime for an awesome eight-hour trek down into the gorge through dingy tunnels and along a series of narrow ledges above the river – not for those with vertigo! Both car trails take approximately half a day, ending at Moustiers-Ste-Marie (▶ 74).

6

Montagne Ste-Victoire

Paul Cézanne was so fascinated by Mont Ste-Victoire that he painted it over 65 times, making this great Provençal landmark famous world-wide.

The Montagne Ste-Victoire lies just east of Aix-en-Provence. This 16km long silvery ridge running east-west which, viewed end on, takes the form of a shapely pyramid. On its lower red-soil slopes, Coteaux-d'Aix vineyards give way to dense forest, scrub and fragrant herbs. Above the tree line, the limestone peak reflects every hue of light and shadow – blue, grey, white, pink, orange – creating extraordinary designs on the landscape.

✚ 69A2

ℹ Aix-en Provence Tourist Office: 2 place Général-de-Gaulle (☎ 04 42 16 11 61)

↔ Aix-en-Provence (▶ 52)

For Paul Cézanne, native of Aix, the mountain was his favourite local subject. He painted it again and again from all angles and at all hours, creating some of his greatest canvases including *La Montagne Sainte-Victoire* (1904) and *Le Paysage d'Aix* (1905). In a letter to his son in 1906, he wrote 'I spend every day in this landscape, with its beautiful shapes. Indeed, I cannot imagine a more pleasant way or place to pass my time'.

Climbing Mont Ste-Victoire requires stout shoes and sure-footedness as, although not the highest mountain in Provence, it is said to be the steepest. It is a steady two-hour hike from Les Cabassols to the ruined 17th-century priory and massive Croix de Provence at the 945m summit. At the base of the mountain is Pourrières, where the mountain was named following a mighty Roman victory over invading Teuton hordes.

Cézanne's beloved mountain can be seen for miles around

21

7
Musée Matisse, Nice

✉ 164 avenue des Arènes de Cimiez

✚ 85B2

A truly remarkable collection of Matisse's works, intimate yet instructive and spanning his entire life, housed in a vivid red villa.

Matisse's masterpiece The Rocaille Armchair, *1946*

☎ 04 93 81 08 08

🕐 Apr–Sep, 10–6; Oct–Mar, 10–5. Closed Tue and hols

🍴 Café restaurant

🚌 15, 17, 20, 22, 25

♿ Very good

✋ Expensive

↔ Musée Archéologique (▶ 80), Cimiez Monastery (▶ 80)

❓ Guided tours Wed 3PM except during school holidays. Three temporary exhibitions a year. Shop. Lectures

The villa des Arènes is situated on a hill above Nice, at the heart of a 3.6 hectare olive grove in the district of Cimiez (▶ 80) – an exquisite mid-17th century folly, with a cleverly-painted *tromp-l'oeil* façade, colonnaded staircases and terraces that are laid out in the Genoese style.

Henri Matisse first came to live in Nice in 1917 and spent long periods of his life near here, and shortly before his death in 1954, he bequeathed his entire personal collection to the City of Nice. Together with a second, even larger donation from his wife in 1960 (including over a hundred personal effects from his studio-apartment in the nearby Hôtel Regina) it formed the basis of a priceless collection, celebrating the life, work and influence of this great artist, and boasting not only the world's largest collection of his drawings, but also all the bronze sculptures that Matisse ever made.

Matisse's entire working life is displayed in the villa, from the initial Old Master copies he made during his apprenticeship period, through an era of sober, dark-toned paintings in the 1890s (including *Intérieur à l'harmonium*), to his Impressionist and Fauvist phases (*Jeune femme à l'ombrelle* and *Portrait of Madame Matisse*) and beyond to the bright colours and simple shapes of his maturity, best protrayed in his decorative paper cut-outs, silk-screen hangings, and works such as *Nu Bleu IV* and *Nature Morte aux Grenades*.

The large collection of his drawings and engravings (around 450 altogether) are also of particular interest, especially the book illustrations for James Joyce's *Ulysses*, and the powerful sketches and stained-glass models for the Chapelle du Rosaire at Vence (▶ 90) should definitely not be missed.

8
Musée Picasso, Antibes

Picasso once had a studio inside this old, seafront castle. Today it houses one of the world's finest collections of his works.

The Grimaldi dynasty ruled for centuries in this beautiful 13th- to 16th-century château, constructed following the design of an ancient Roman fort and occupying a strategic site overlooking the ramparts. In 1928, the City of Antibes acquired the castle to house a Museum of Art, History and Archaeology. When in 1946, Pablo Picasso returned to his beloved Mediterranean, having spent the war years in Paris, he found that he had nowhere suitable to work. The Mayor of Antibes lent him a room in Château Grimaldi for use as an *atelier* and, in gratitude, Picasso left his entire output of that period on permanent loan to the castle museum, together with a collection of lively ceramics, tapestries and sculptures which he later created in the nearby village of Vallauris. More of his work can be seen in the two museums there.

Although Picasso only spent six months in Antibes, it was one of his most prolific periods. After the melancholy of war, his work here took on a new dimension, reflecting the *joie de vivre* of the Mediterranean, bathed in sunny colours and incandescent light. He combined bold new techniques – using industrial paints, fibrecement and plywood – with ancient themes and mythical images, creating such masterpieces as *Le centaur et le Navire*, *Ulysee et les Sirènes*, *Nu couché au lit bleu* and his famous *La Joie de Vivre*.

Most of Picasso's works can be found on the first floor of the castle. Works by his contemporaries, including Léger, Modigliani and Max Ernst, hang on the second floor (Picasso's former studio), and the ground floor contains photographs of the great master at work. On a sunny terrace overlooking the sea, stone and bronze sculptures by Miró, Richier and Pagès are strikingly displayed among cacti, trees and flowers.

 85A2

 Château Grimaldi

 04 92 90 54 20

 Jun–Sep, 10–6; Oct–May, 10–12, 2–6. Closed Mon and public hols

 Expensive

 Biot (►84), Cagnes (►84), Cannes (►85), Mougins (►89)

? Guided tours on request. Children's workshops (phone for details)

Picasso's bold and innovative use of line and colour can be seen at the Picasso Museum

9

Roussillon

✚ 39B1

ℹ Roussillon Tourist
Office: place de la Poste
(☎ 04 90 05 60 25)

🍴 David (➤ 93)

♿ Good (lower village);
few (upper village)

↔ Gordes (➤ 19); villages
of the Lubéron (➤ 38)

❓ Ochre festival held in
May (during Ascension
weekend)

It is easy to fall in love with Roussillon, once known world-wide for its ochre dyes, now considered one of France's most beautiful villages.

This unforgettable village is perched on a platform of rich rust rock called Mont Rouge, surrounded by jagged cliffs and hollows of every shade of ochre imaginable from blood red, gold, orange and pale yellow to white, pink and violet, hidden amidst dark green pine forests and scrub. For here lie the richest deposits of ochre in all France.

The village of Roussillon was founded by Raymond d'Avignon. According to legend, one day he discovered his wife was having an affair with his pageboy. He killed the page and served his heart on a platter to his wife. Greatly distressed, she leapt off the cliffs, and her blood formed a spring, permanently colouring the surrounding soil and creating some of the most spectacular scenery in the whole of Provence, from the spiky multi-coloured needles of the 'Valley of Fairies' to the brilliantly hued 'Cliffs of

Blood' and deep gullies of the 'Giant's Causeway'. Here visitors can explore the old opencast quarries along the 1km *Sentier des Ocres* (Ochre Trail) which has information signboards along the way.

The ochre industry began here at the end of the 18th century, bringing prosperity to the villagers until 1958, when competition from cheap synthetic pigments forced production to stop. Although today very few quarries are still excavated, Roussillon still holds its merry Ochre Festival at Ascensiontide.

The picturesque houses present a full palette of ochre shades – apricot, pink, violet, gold, mustard, orange, burgundy, russet and brown – creating a special glow in the streets. The hub of the village is the small, lively square beside the *Mairie*, where the *Roussillonais* gather in the outdoor cafés. Narrow lanes and winding stairways lead up to a Romanesque church, offering a sweeping panorama of the ochreous Vaucluse scenery, with its hill villages and distant mountains.

The Sentier des Ocres *is a must for visitors to Roussillon*

10
Théâtre Antique, Orange

✝ 39A2

✉ place des Frères-Mounet

☎ 04 90 51 17 10

🕐 Apr–Sep, 9–6:30; Oct–Mar, 9–12, 1:30–5. Closed 25 Dec, 1 Jan

♿ Restricted

✋ Expensive, but also valid for Musée Municipal

↔ Musée de la Ville (► 44)

❓ Guided tours at 10:30 Jul–Aug. Telephone for concert and theatre details

One of the best surviving ancient theatres in the world, built over 2,000 years ago, with seating for up to 10,000 spectators.

The Antique Theatre was built in the reign of Augustus around AD1, set into the hillside of Colline Saint-Eutrope at Arausio. Originally there had been a Celtic settlement here, but under Caesar, veterans of the second Gallica legion created a major Roman city, building the magnificent theatre, the triumphal arch, temples, baths and many other public buildings.

Although all that remains of the theatre is a mere shadow of its former splendour, it is nevertheless easy to imagine the theatre in its heyday. The *cavea*, or tiered semicircle, was divided into three levels according to rank. On one tier you can still see the inscription *EQ GIII* meaning 'Equus Gradus III' or third row for knights! Senators and guests of honour would occupy marble seats in front of the first row.

The monumental stage wall (*frons scanae*), made from red sandstone and measuring 103m long, 37m high and nearly 2m thick, is the only one in the world to survive completely from ancient times. Louis XIV described it as 'the greatest wall in my kingdom'! Once decorated with 76 columns, friezes, niches and statues, today all the statues have vanished except an imposing marble figure of Emperor Augustus.

Perched high above the stage, it is easy to step back to Roman times

Beneath the statue is the central 'Royal door', and within the wall were hidden passageways enabling actors and stagehands to move about unseen. For the same purpose the wooden stage had numerous trap doors. In Roman times the theatre was used for meetings, lectures, theatre and concerts. Its excellent acoustics are demonstrated every July and August in the 'Chorégies', a world-famous festival of opera, drama and ballet, held here since 1869. Classical, jazz and pop concerts are also held here throughout the summer.

To the west of the theatre, Colline St-Eutrope is well worth the climb to reach its cool, shady park with magnificent views over Orange, the theatre and the Rhône plain beyond.

What To See

PROVENCE

Mauve corduroy fields of lavender stripe the landscape

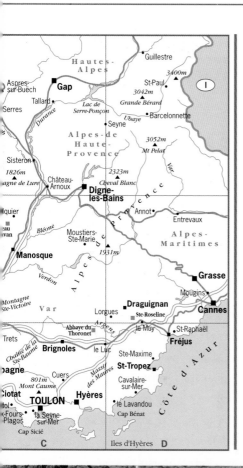

Hautes-Alpes

• Guillestre

Aspres-sur-Buëch

■ **Gap**

3400m ▲

St-Paul

Tallard •

Lac de Serre-Ponçon

3042m ▲
Grande Bérard

Serres

Durance

• Barcelonnette
Ubaye

Sisteron

• Seyne

Alpes-de-Haute-Provence

1826m ▲
agne de Lure

Château-Arnoux ■

3052m ▲
Mt Pelat

Var

|quier

2323m ▲
Cheval Blanc

■ **Digne-les-Bains**

au
van

Bléone

Annot •

• Entrevaux

■ **Manosque**

Moustiers-Ste-Marie

1931m ▲

Alpes-Maritimes

Verdon

Alpes de Provence

■ **Grasse**

Montagne Ste-Victoire

Var

Mougins •

■ **Draguignan**

Lorgues •
Ste-Roseline ■

■ **Cannes**

Trets

Abbaye du Thoronet ■
Argens
le Muy •

• St-Raphaël

Brignoles ■
le Luc •

■ **Fréjus**

Chaîne de la Ste-Baume

Ste-Maxime •

agne

Cuers •

Massif des Maures

■ **St-Tropez**

801m ▲
Mont Caume

St-Tropez ■

Cavalaire-sur-Mer •

iotat

TOULON ■

■ **Hyères**

Côte d'Azur

tol
x-Fours-Plages •
la Seyne-sur-Mer •

le Lavandou •
Cap Bénat

Cap Sicié

Iles d'Hyères **D**

C

Vaucluse

Despite being one of France's smallest *départements*, the Vaucluse has been blessed with more than its fair share of beautiful scenery and treasures. A region of colourful, bustling markets, swift-flowing rivers, sweetly-scented *garrigue*, brilliant red and yellow ochre cliffs, and world-famous wines. The timeless quality of its sunbleached landscapes are reinforced by some of the finest Roman remains in the world at Orange and Vaison-la-Romaine, and the entire region is saturated in medieval antiquities, from the remotest *village perché* to the papal grandeur of Avignon.

For many the Lubéron region epitomises the real magic of Provence – timeless villages dozing under blue skies, ornamental fountains splashing in the sleepy squares and villagers playing boules under shady plane trees or enjoying a simple meal whilst gazing out over silvery olive groves, scented fig trees and neat rows of lavender.

'It is a land of milk and honey, the best milk and the most perfumed honey, where all the good things of the earth overflow and are cooked to perfection.'

WILLIAM BOLITHO
(*Camera Obscura*)

Avignon

The city of Avignon – administrative centre of the Vaucluse and a major artistic centre – is one of the most important cities in the history of France. Strategically located near the junction of the Rhône and Durance rivers, it has been the scene of countless conflicts since Roman times, and for over a century it was the seat of the popes and centre of a religious and political power struggle.

It was a French pope, Clement V, who first moved his residence from the Vatican to Avignon in 1309. From then on, a succession of French popes and cardinals built up a powerful base here, constructing a cornucopia of architectural treasures within the city's massive fortifications to display their wealth and power. Following pressure from the rest of Europe, the papal establishment finally transferred back to Rome in 1377. However, a group of French cardinals refused to accept this, and elected a series of rival 'anti-popes' who, over the next 40 years, continued to exercise authority from Avignon, creating what is today known as the Great Schism.

A walk along the ramparts reveals the two sides of Avignon today – the village-like atmosphere of the historic old walled town, its skyline adorned with steeples and monuments, and the sprawling factories and bustling modern suburbs beyond, accommodating the city's 100,000 inhabitants. It is a cheerful, lively tourist centre, especially in July when the narrow lanes and pedestrian zones resound with buskers, street theatre and café cabarets during the renowned Arts Festival (▶ 60).

The Palais des Papes, an imposing sight above the river

🞢 32B2
✉ 5 rue Laboureur
☎ 04 90 82 29 03
🕓 Nov–Apr, 1–6; May–Oct,
1–7. Closed Mon–Tue all
year
💷 Expensive

🞢 32B2
✉ 65 rue Joseph Vernet

*Avignon's main square,
the Place de l'Horloge,
is always a lively meeting-
point*

ℹ Avignon Tourist Office:
41 Cours Jean Jaurés
(☎ 04 90 82 65 11)
↔ Carpentras (➤ 40);
Cavaillon (➤ 41);
Châteauneuf-du-Pape
(➤ 35); Orange (➤ 44);
Tarascon (➤ 58)

What to See in Avignon

FONDATION ANGLADON DUBRUJEAUD ✪✪

This new museum in an elegant city mansion boasts the prestigious collection of artists Jean and Paulette Angladon-Dubrujeaud, including paintings by Sisley, Manet, Cézanne and Picasso and Provence's only original Van Gogh.

MUSÉE CALVET ✪

The private art collection of physician Dr Esprit Calvet (1728–1810) provides a comprehensive study of the

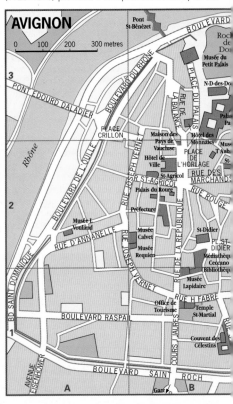

French and Avignon schools of painting and sculpture from the 14th to 20th centuries, including works by David, Delacroix, Modigliani and Manet.

☎ 04 90 86 33 84
🕐 10–1, 2–6 (7 in summer)
♿ Good 💷 Expensive

MUSÉE ROURE ✪

Until the end of the last century, this Florentine-style palace was the office of Frédérick Mistral's Provençal-language magazine *L'Aïoli*. Today it is a beautiful museum of Provençal history, arts, literature and traditions.

✚ 32B2
✉ 3 rue Collège du Roure
☎ 04 90 80 80 88
🕐 Tue at 3PM or by appt
♿ Few 💷 Free

PLACE DE L'HORLOGG ✪✪

A lively square, abuzz with cafés, artists and buskers.

✚ 32B2

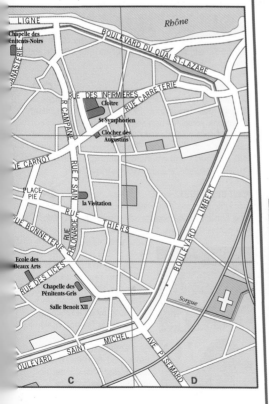

The shady gardens of the Rochers des Doms offer a cool retreat for a picnic

32B3
place du Palais
04 90 27 50 71
Nov–Mar, 9–12:45, 2–6;
Apr–Oct, 9–7 (festival
9–9); 5 Aug–30 Sep, 9–8
Café in summer months
Few
Very expensive
Petit Palais (▶ below)
Guided tours only ☎ 04
90 27 50 73/74

PALAIS DES PAPES

The majestic, monumental Pope's Palace was built in a spacious cobbled square as a symbol of the papal residency in Avignon. Its massive walls shelter a labyrinth of halls, courtyards and chambers divided into the 'Old Palace', built by Pope Benoit XII between 1334 and 1342, and the 'New Palace', begun under his successor, Pope Clement VI and completed in 1348. Each part has its own distinctive character. Benoit XII's old palace has an almost austere, monastic simplicity in stark contrast with the new palace.

Clement VI enjoyed the high life and was an ardent patron of the arts, displaying his wealth and power in lavish frescoes and flamboyant ceilings. This ostentatious new palace received a mixed reception. Medieval chronicler, Froissart, pronounced it 'the finest and strongest palace in the world' whereas Petrach called it 'Unholy Babylon.... a sewer where all the filth of the universe has gathered'. The entire complex is so vast that it has been described as 'a city within a city', and takes at least a day to visit. Don't miss the fanciful Audience Hall, the frescoes of the Stag Room, the princely papal bedroom, St Martial's Chapel and the Hall of the Consistory.

32B3
place du Palais
04 90 86 44 58
Wed–Mon 9:30–12, 2–6.
Closed Tue. Jul–Aug 10–6.
Few Moderate (free
Sun Oct–Mar)
Palais des Papes
(▶ above)

PETIT PALAIS

A beautifully-restored former residence of the bishops of Avignon was converted in 1958 to house two important collections – medieval works from the Calvet Museum and the Campana collection of 13th- to 16th-century Italian paintings from the Louvre. The medieval works include 600 sculptures and around 60 paintings, such as the Requien Altarpiece by Enguerrand Quarton.

32B3
rue Ferruce
04 90 85 60 16
Nov–Feb, daily 9–1, 2–5
except Mon; Oct & Mar,
daily 9–1, 2–5; Apr–Sep,
daily 9–6:30. Closed 25
Dec, 1 Jan, 1 May and 14
Jul
None Moderate
Petit Palais (▶ above);
Rocher des Doms (▶ 33)

PONT ST BÉNÉZET

This famous bridge, immortalised in the popular children's song Sur le pont d'Avignon, was one of the first bridges built across the Rhône. Originally made of wood, it was

reconstructed in stone at the end of the 13th century. Today only four of its original 22 arches remain, together with the tiny chapel of St Nicholas on the second pier. The song by an anonymous composer is famous world-wide. However it was under the arches of the bridge (sous le pont), on the Île de la Barthelasse, that the people of Avignon used to dance.

'Sur le pont d'Avignon, on y danse, on y danse...'

*The rolling vineyards of
Beaumes-de-Venise*

Côtes du Rhône Villages

The stony, sun-baked red-clay soil of the southern Rhône nurtures some of France's most prestigious wines – fine and full-bodied with a spicy bouquet, of which the best-known is Châteauneuf-du-Pape. Numerous wine routes lead you through charming yellowstone villages with shady squares, old fountains and red-tiled roofs, hidden in a sea of vineyards and largely given over to restaurants and cellars offering free wine-tasting.

BEAUMES-DE-VENISE ✪✪

Majestically framed by the lacy silver crags of the Dentelles de Montmirail, Beaumes is well-known for its sweet golden Muscat wines. Taste them at the Cave des Vignerons or during the annual summer Wine Festival, accompanied by goats' cheeses, *foie gras* and melons drowned in Muscat.

🔾 39B2
ℹ️ Tourist Office: cours Jean Jaurès, 84190 Beaumes-de-Venise (☎ 04 90 62 94 39)
🔁 Carpentras (➤ 40)
❓ Wine festival: mid Aug

CHÂTEAUNEUF-DU-PAPE ✪✪✪

The wines of Châteauneuf-du-Pape are world-renowned, largely thanks to 13th-century Pope Jean XXII of Avignon. It was he who built the now-ruined château, with its splendid views, as a summer residence and planted the first vineyards. Many Côtes du Rhône wines are made from just one grape variety, but vintners here blend up to 13 different grapes to produce their distinctive wines of unique complexity. The Musée du Père Anselme here is dedicated to the history of local viticulture and visitors can indulge in wine tastings.

🔾 39A2
ℹ️ Tourist Office: place du Portail (☎ 04 90 83 71 08)
🔁 Orange (➤ 44)
❓ Wine festival: early Aug

GIGONDAS ✪✪

The wines of this small, unspoilt village, set against the jagged backdrop of the Dentelles, are reputed to be the best in the area, notably the intense red Grenache wines.

🔾 39B2
ℹ️ Tourist Office: place du Portail, 84190 Gigondas (☎ 04 90 65 85 46)
❓ Wine festival: mid Aug

SÉGURET ✪✪✪

This charming circular hilltop village has its own individual *appellation contrôlée*. The ochre cottages, with their turquoise shutters hidden behind vines and creeper, house craftsmen renowned for their dried flowers and *santons* (terracotta Christmas crib figurines).

🔾 39B2
✉️ Tourist Office: Vaison-la-Romaine, place du Chanoine Sautel (☎ 04 90 36 02 11)
🔁 Vaison-la-Romaine (➤ 45)

Food & Drink

France is universally recognised as the world leader in the field of food and wine, and of all its great regional styles *la cuisine Provençale* has one of the strongest personalities; spicy Mediterranean dishes with bold, sun-drenched flavours as varied as its landscapes, leaning heavily on olive oil, tomatoes, garlic and wild herbs. As Peter Mayle remarked: 'Everything is full-blooded. The food is full of strong, earthy flavours... There is nothing bland about Provence.' (*A Year in Provence*)

HERBES DE PROVENCE

Provençal specialities include *soupe au pistou* (vegetable soup with garlic, basil and cheese); *beignets de courgettes* (courgette flowers dipped in batter and deep fried), *mesclun* (a hearty salad including dandelion and hedge-mustard leaves), *daube* (beef stew with red wine, cinnamon and lemon peel), *salade Niçoise* (with tuna, egg, black olives and anchovies) and *pain bagnat* (Niçoise salad inside a loaf of bread).

Cuisine Niçoise

Within the Provençal tradition, the Nice area has its own distinctive cuisine, reflecting the town's former association

Aix-en-Provence's markets are famous throughout the region

with Italy. Indeed, pizzas and pastas taste every bit as good in Menton and Nice as they do over the border. Look out also for *pissaladière* (olive and onion pizza), *socca* (thin pancake made of chickpea flour), *petits farcis* (savoury stuffed artichoke hearts, courgettes and tomatoes) and *estocaficada* (stockfish stew).

Surf and Turf

Near the coast, fish dishes reign supreme. Expect to pay at least F250 for an authentic *bouillabaisse* (▶ 95), or else try *bourride*, poor man's fish soup. *Moules frites* (mussels with french fries) are always good value, as are *tellines Camarguais*, tiny shellfish served with *aïoli* (garlic mayonnaise). By contrast inland, meat dishes predominate. Try Sisteron lamb with its taste of wild thyme, game dishes, *boeuf gardian* (a spicy beef stew with olives, served with Camarguais rice) or frogs legs *à la Provençale* (in a tomato and garlic sauce). And don't forget the tasty mountain cheeses, lavender-scented honey and truffles.

Vin de Provence

Eleven per cent of France's wine comes from Provence. The chalky soils and warm dry Mediterranean climate lend themselves to the development of the smooth, easy-to-drink wines such as *Côtes du Ventoux* and *Côtes du Lubéron*. Some of the more famous labels include *Côtes du Rhône* (▶ 35), notably *Gigondas*, *Vacqueyras* and *Châteauneuf-du-Pape* – a full-bodied, robust wine with a powerful, complex bouquet, perfect with red meats and cheeses.

Provence is particularly famous for its rosé wines, fresh, crisp and fruity, and an ideal accompaniment to seafood. *Côtes de Provence* and *Côteaux d'Aix* are numbered among the best. For a white wine, try the dry, green-tinged *Cassis* wines (▶ 94) or the fruity white *Bellet*, one of Provence's most original wines and, with only 20 producers, much prized by connoisseurs (▶ 109). Other specialist wines of the region include *Listel*, a cloudy 'grey' rosé and the golden, sultana-flavoured dessert wine, *Muscat de Beaumes de Venise* (▶ 35).

Some of Provence's best wines come from the Lubéron near Menerbes

Sweet Things
For those with a sweet tooth there are juicy Cavaillon melons, *pain d'épice* (spiced bread), delicious crystalised fruits and a medley of candies including burnt-sugar *Berlingots* from Carpentras and *Calissons d'Aix*. In 1994, the village of Sault entered the Guinness Book of Records with the world's biggest bag of nougat, 3m high and filled with 40,000 pieces!

🕂 40C1
Parc Naturel Régional du Lubéron
✉ Maison du Parc, 1 place Jean-Jaurès
🕓 Mon–Sat, 8:30–12, 1:30–6 (till 7 Apr–Sep)

🕂 40C1
ℹ Apt Tourist Office: place Bouquerie (☎ 04 90 74 03 18)
↔ Roussillon (► 24)

A small fountain in central Apt

🕂 40B1
ℹ Bonnieux Touristt Office: 7 place Carnot (☎ 04 90 75 91 90)
↔ Lacoste (► 43)

The Lubéron

The Parc Naturel Régional du Lubéron is a protected region of cedar and pine-clad countryside interspersed with lavender fields, almond and olive groves, fragrant herbs, *garrigue* scrub and vineyards, draped across a compact range of small mountains which stretch from Cavaillon to Manosque.

The dramatic wooded gorge of the Combe de Lourmarin (road D943) splits the region in two. The high, wild mountains the Grand Lubéron lie to the east. Walkers tackling the strenuous climb from Auribeau to the uppermost peak of Mourre Nègre (1,100m) will be well-rewarded with dizzy-making views from the Basse-Alpes to the Mediterranean. To the west, the pretty *villages perchés* of the Petit Lubéron have long been one of France's most fashionable *residences secondaires*, even before Peter Mayle's bestseller *A Year in Provence*!

APT
This busy old market town north of the Lubéron Mountains makes an ideal centre for touring the area. The best place to start is at the Maison du Parc Naturel Régional du Luberon, which details walks and other outdoor activities, together with a small museum documenting local natural history.

The town itself is surrounded by fruit trees. Hardly surprisingly, it is renowned for its jams and claims to be the 'world capital of crystallized fruit'! Try some for yourself along with other tempting Provençal specialities at the bustling Saturday market; always a jolly affair with barrel organs and buskers. Apt is also well known for its lavender essence, hand-made pottery and is an important centre for the truffle trade in winter.

BONNIEUX
The terracotta-roofed houses of Bonnieux wind their way up to a tiny 12th-century chapel surrounded by sentinel-like cypresses. The village is spread out on a north-facing spur of the Petit Lubéron overlooking the vineyards, cherry trees and lavender fields of the Coulon valley, and its belvedere commands entrancing views over the Vaucluse Plateau to mighty Mont Ventoux beyond. Once a papal fief, Bonnieux has preserved many fine monuments including the Town Hall, a Bakery Museum and some notable Renaissance paintings in its two churches.

GORDES (► 19, TOP TEN)

LOURMARIN ○○
The imposing Renaissance castle, the medieval houses made from local yellow stone and dressed in honeysuckle, tiny fountain-filled squares and a host of inviting restaurants create a picturesque ensemble on the southern slopes of the Lubéron. French novelist and philosopher Albert Camus bought a house here after winning the Nobel prize for literature in 1957. His simple grave can be visited in the village cemetery.

✚ 40C1
🛈 Lourmarin Tourist Office: avenue Philippe de Girard (☎ 04 90 68 10 77)
↔ Bonnieux (► 38)

MÉNERBES ○○
The Luberón's highest-profile village, has long attracted celebrities including Picasso's mistress Dora Maar, and more recently Mitterand and Peter Mayle. Sadly, this scenic, once off-the-beaten-track village, perched high above neat rows of vines in the Petit Lubéron, has suffered from its association with Mayle (who lived in a *mas* near by until he was driven away by hoards of visiting fans!) Nevertheless, it remains a lively, working village with a dynamic weekly market, 13th-century fortress and 14th-century church.

✚ 40B1
🛈 No tourist office. Contact Bonnieux Tourist Office (► 38)
 Good
↔ Oppéde-le-Vieux (► 39), Bonnieux (► 38), Lacoste (► 43)

OPPÈDE-LE-VIEUX ○○
At first glimpse, Oppède appears a typical Provençal village of narrow streets, stairways and attractive, cream-coloured houses tumbling down the hillside, all crowned by an impressive ruined château. On closer inspection, you will see that many of the houses are gutted ruins, overrun with weeds. The village was abandoned late last century, following the tyrannical reign of Baron Oppède who sold over 800 villagers as slaves in Marseille. Recently, some of the quaint old cottages and the Romanesque church have been restored by resident artists and Oppède is gradually returning to its former glory.

✚ 40B1
↔ Cavaillon (► 35), Menerbes (► 40)

Beautiful Bonnieux tumbles down the hillside in the Petit Lúberon

What else to See in Vaucluse

CARPENTRAS ✪

🗺 40B2

ℹ Carpentras Tourist Office: allée Jean-Jaurés (☎ 04 90 63 57 88)

↔ Côtes du Rhône villages (▶ 35), Orange (▶ 44), Vaison-la-Romaine (▶ 45), Venasque (▶ 45)

Cathédrale St-Siffrein

✉ place Générale de Gaulle

☎ 04 90 63 08 33

Synagogue

✉ place de la Mairie

☎ 04 90 63 39 97

🕐 Mon–Thu 10–12, 3–5, Fri 10–12, 3–4. Closed during hols

This prosperous market town, at the heart of the Côtes-du-Ventoux wine region, was the old capital of Venasque (then called the Comtat Venaissin) from the 14th century until the Revolution. Situated beside the River Auzon in the midst of rich farmland, it is well-known throughout the region for its Friday morning market, when the shady plane-tree lined avenues of the old town are filled with the colours and fragrances of Provence alongside Carpentras' own specialities – truffles, candied fruits and the stripy boiled sweets called *berlingots*.

In the heart of town, a small triumphal arch with vivid carvings of chained prisoners marks the Roman era at Carpentras, whereas the nearby Porte d'Orange is the only surviving part of the medieval ramparts. Other notable buildings include the Gothic **Cathédrale St-Siffrein** and France's oldest **synagogue**, which dates back to 1327.

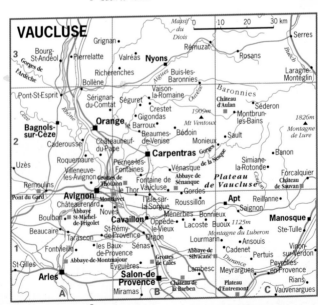

CAVAILLON ✪

Cavaillon is France's greatest market garden – its very name synonymous with those delicious, sweet, pink-fleshed melons – and boasts one of Europe's largest wholesale fruit and vegetable markets. The vast, mouth-watering weekly market for the general public every Monday morning is considered the most important market in the Vaucluse.

The town's agricultural wealth stems from its location in the highly fertile Durance valley. From the Colline St-Jacques, a former neolithic site at the top of the town, there are spectacular views across the valley to the distant highlands of the Luberon and the Alpilles. Back in the town centre, numerous Roman finds have been assembled in the Musée Archéologique. The former cathedral is also worth visiting, as is the beautifully preserved 18th-century synagogue, with its small museum illustrating the region's traditional protection of Jewish communities.

FONTAINE-DE-VAUCLUSE ✪✪✪

Tucked away at the end of the narrow, enclosed *Vallis Clausa* valley, after which the whole Vaucluse *département* is named, Fontaine-de-Vaucluse is famous for an emerald-green spring, which gushes from a huge cave-like abyss at the foot of a 230m cliff. Recent research has proved that this is one of the world's largest and most powerful springs, consisting of a vast underground labyrinth of rivers covering over 2,000sq km, able to produce up to 200,000 litres of water per second at certain times of year. Pagan Gauls believed it to be the home of a god, while Christians named it the Devil's Hole.

Fontaine's other main tourist attractions include a **paper mill**, the last of a once thriving industry, and a small **museum** which is dedicated to the famous 14th-century Italian poet Petrarch. He wrote most of his poetry during a 16-year stay here, inspired by the solitude and wilderness he found in the valley.

🔲 40B1

ℹ️ Cavaillon Tourist Office: 79 rue Saunerie (☎ 04 90 71 32 01)

🔄 Oppède-le-Vieux (▶ 39), Fontaine-de-Vaucluse (▶ 41), Eygalières (▶ 56), Gordes (▶ 19)

Below: Tranquil Fontaine-de-Vaucluse, on the River Sorgue

🔲 40B2

ℹ️ Fontaine-De-Vaucluse Tourist Office: chemin de la Fontaine (☎ 04 90 20 32 22)

Moulin à Paper Vallis Clausa
✉️ chemin de Gouffre
☎ 04 90 20 31 72
🕐 Daily. Closed 1 Jan, 25 Dec

Musée Petrach
✉️ Rive Gauche de la Sorgue
☎ 04 90 20 37 20
🕐 Mid Apr–mid Oct, Wed–Mon 10–12, 2–6:30; mid Oct–Dec & Mar–mid Apr, Sat–Sun

📍 40B2

ℹ️ Mont Ventoux
Information: Chalet
d'Accueil du Mont
Ventoux (☎ 04 90 63 42
02)

↔️ Carpentras (▶ 40),
Vaison-la-Romaine (▶ 45)

❓ Organised hikes with
Rando-Ventoux Centre
Régional de la
Randonnée (☎ 04 90 65
63 95 – Bedoin Tourist
Office) to the summit for
sunrise

MONT VENTOUX ✪✪

The awesome, isolated massif of Mont Ventoux – the
'Giant of Provence' – rises a lofty 1,901m above the
Plateau of Vaucluse, making it the highest peak between
the Alps and the Pyrenees. Italian poet Francesco Petrarch
was the first man to reach its summit in 1336. It is a good
4–5-hour hike, but today most people 'cheat' and drive up
to the Col des Tempêtes (1,829m). It is important to wrap
up warm because Mont Ventoux (Provençal for 'windy
mountain') does justice to its name. Its bleak limestone
peak, totally devoid of vegetation, has been blasted white
by icy *mistral* winds of up to 250kph. For much of the year,
the summit is snow-clad, and skiing on its slopes is a
popular pastime.

You'll find a game of
boules in action in most
shady squares

Did you know ?

*Boules, Southern France's most popular game,
is called pétanque in Provence, from Occitan pé
('foot') and tanco ('fixed to the ground').
The game was born one day in 1901 when
arthritic boules player, Jules Le Noir, suggested
to his friends that they all play pieds tanqués.
This seemed a good idea and also meant they
could return to the village square where they had
been previously banned for hitting too many
passers'by as they ran and tossed their balls!
Pétanque is a tactical game – whether to
position your ball near the little wooden ball
(called a cochonnet or 'piglet') or to oust out your
opponent's ball. With a flick of the wrist, top
players sometimes manage both simultaneously.*

A Drive Around The Luberon

Starting in Apt, take the D22 north-east towards Rustrel, then right at the crossroads to Bouvene.

The enormous old ochre quarries of Colorado de Rustrel are a colourful tourist attraction – an almost lunar landscape of mounds, pillars, cliffs and hollows in every imaginable shade of ochre from pale yellow to blood red, set against deep pine forest. (From Bouvene it is a 50-minute walk).

Back at the crossroads, continue straight on along the D179 then the D943 to St Saturnin-les-Apt. Leave the village on the D2 to Gordes (➤ 19). After Gordes, continue along the D2 towards Cavaillon, then take the first left (D103) signposted Apt and Les Beaumettes. Go straight on at the roundabout, following signs up to the centre of Ménerbes (➤ 39).

Outside Ménerbes, the Domaine de la Citadelle has a unique museum of corkscrews (Musée du Tire-Bouchon) dating back to the 17th century, along with complimentary wine tasting.

Leave Ménerbes on the D103 then the D109 past the Renaissance abbey of St-Hilaire to Lacoste.

Lacoste vies with neighbouring villages Ménerbes, Bonnieux and Oppède for the title of prettiest Lubéron village – a 'film-set' village perché, rich, exclusive and crowned by an 11th-century château which in its heyday was one of the region's grandest.

Further along the D109 you reach Bonnieux (➤ 38). Leave the village on the D3, then first left (D149) to Pont Julien.

Lubéron farm and vineyards

This bridge is reputedly the best-preserved Roman bridge in France.

Turn right at the main road (N100) for the return journey to Apt.

Distance
90 km

Time
2½ hours without stops; full day with visits

Start/end point
Apt
➕ 40C1

Lunch
Le Simiane, Lacoste (££)
✉ rue Sous-Barri
☎ 04 90 75 83 31

🔲 40A2
ℹ️ Tourist Office: 5 cours
Aristide Briand (☎ 04 90
34 70 88)
↔️ Carpentras (➤ 40),
Châteauneuf-du-Pape
(➤ 35), Côtes du Rhône
villages (➤ 35), Vaison-la-
Romaine (➤ 45)

Arc de Triomphe
✉️ avenue de l'Arc de
Triomphe/N7

Municipal Museum
✉️ rue Madeleine-Roch
☎ 04 90 51 18 24
🕐 Apr–Sep 9–7, Sun
9:30–7; Oct–Mar 9–12,
1:30–5:30
♿ Good
🖐️ Expensive
↔️ Théâtre Antique (➤ 26)

*The ancient arch stands
majestically in the midst
of modern Orange*

ORANGE ✪✪

Historical Orange, the 'Gateway to Provence', lies in the
fertile plain of the River Rhône. Once the Celtic capital of
Arausio, later colonised by veterans of the Roman Second
Legion, its present name dates from the 16th century,
when the town became the property of the House of
Orange. Its main claim to fame are two of the finest
Roman monuments in Europe – the great triumphal arch
and the massive theatre. Today Orange is an important
centre for Côtes du Rhône wines and produce such as
olives, honey and truffles.

The massive 22-m **Arc de Triomphe** was the first
Roman monument to be built on Gallic soil around 20 BC. It
was constructed following Caesar's conquest of the Gauls
and victory over the Greek fleet as a symbol of Roman
power, and its three archways are smothered with
intricate carvings depicting naked Gauls bound in chains,
victorious Roman legionaries and a variety of nautical
symbols portraying maritime supremacy. Originally
constructed along the Via Agrippa from Lyons to Arles,
today it stands on a roundabout in the middle of the N7
Route Nationale.

The **Municipal Museum** gives a detailed insight into
life in Roman Gaul. The most remarkable exhibit is a huge
marble slab, pieced together from over 400 fragments to
create a *plan cadastral* (land survey) of the region, detailing
boundaries, land owners and tax rates. There is also a full
history of the city and some interesting portraits of the
Royal House of Orange. The museum is a splendid introduction to the **Théâtre Antique** (➤ 26).

ROUSSILLON (➤ 24, TOP TEN)

VAISON-LA-ROMAINE ✪✪✪

Undisputedly one of Provence's best-preserved Roman sites, Vaison is an extraordinary blend of 'modern town', medieval village and former Roman city, *Vasio Vocontiorum*. The richness of its past only emerged this century, when excavations unearthed extensive Roman remains including the vast Maison des Messii, with its colonnaded courtyard and mosaic floors, and a Roman theatre (seating 7,000 people during the July arts festival). Visit the Roman City before crossing the 2,000 year old Pont Romain over the jade-green River Ouvèze.

Clinging to a lofty jagged rock above the river, the sand-coloured houses of Vaison's medieval village, draped with knotted vines, creeper and pomegranate bushes, have recently been lovingly restored by artists and craftsmen. It is a steep climb to the ruined 13th-century château through a maze of twisting cobbled streets, rewarded by sweeping views across Ouvèze Valley and the Côtes du Rhône vineyards as far as the snow-peaked Alps.

🞖 40B2
🖂 Fouilles de Puymin, place du Chanoine Sautel
☎ 04 90 36 02 11
🕓 Jun–Aug, daily 9–12:30, 2–6:45; Mar–May & Sep–Oct, daily 9:30–12:30, 2–5:40; Nov–Feb, Wed–Mon 10–12, 2–4:30. Closed 1 Jan, 1 May, 25 Dec
♿ Few
🍽 Very expensive
↔ Carpentras (➤ 40), Côtes du Rhône villages (➤ 35), Orange (➤ 44)
❓ Entrance also includes the Musée d'Archéologie, the Cathedral and Cloister

VENASQUE ✪

The lovely ancient village of Venasque, protected by an imposing medieval curtain wall and gateway, enjoys a lofty perch on a steep rock overlooking the Carpentras plain. This formidable site has been occupied since the 6th century, when the bishops of Carpentras sought refuge here from Saracens. It was an episcopal seat for several centuries and a reminder of those times is the remarkable 6th-century **baptistry**, built on the site of a Roman temple dedicated to Venus. The village also has a considerable gastronomic reputation and in May and June, there is a daily cherry market.

🞖 40B2
🛈 Venasque Tourist Office: place de la Mairie (☎ 04 90 66 11 66)
↔ Gordes (➤ 19), Carpentras (➤ 40), Fontaine-de-Vaucluse (➤ 41)

Venasque Baptistière
🖂 place de l'Église
☎ Thu–Tue 10–12, 3–7
🍽 Cheap ❓ Guided tours

Bouches-du-Rhône

Deep rooted in the customs of ancient Provence, this was the home of the Troubadours, where Courtly Love developed. Before that, it was the most important part of the Roman Empire outside Italy. At Arles, Glanum and the Baux the region has preserved its ancient monuments, its beautiful old costumes and its Provençal language.

The entire area is scattered with timeless medieval villages, and honey-coloured farmsteads, drenched in bougainvillea and oleander. The landscape varies dramatically, from the lacy limestone peaks of the Alpilles and Cézanne's immense Mont St Victoire, to Van Gogh's nodding sunflower fields and beyond is the Camargue, a unique nature reserve where pink flamingos, young bulls and herds of white horses inhabit the marshes.

*'I am fascinated with Paris,
its elegance, its women,
even its artificiality.
But with my heart and skin
I love the south —
bullfighting, pleasure, music,
nature, the sea,
goat cheese and bread,
elementary things.'*

CHRISTIAN LACROIX

Arles

After centuries of fame, first as the Roman capital of Provence, then as a major medieval ecclesiastical centre, Arles seemed content to live on its former glory and fine monuments for many years. Recently, however, it has become a lively, popular city, largely due to a variety of new cultural events, including an internationally-renowned photographic fair, a rekindled French passion for bullfighting and the influence of local fashion designer, Christian Lacroix, whose imaginative creations reflect the colourful Arlesian traditional costumes (▶ 105).

For centuries, Arles has attracted artists and writers. The beautiful women of the city inspired Daudet's story *L'Arlésienne*, Bizet's opera of the same name and the *farandole*, a medieval dance. Picasso visited to paint the bullfights, and Van Gogh moved here in 1888 and lived with Gauguin in the famous yellow house (destroyed in the war), which he immortalised on canvas (*La Maison Jaune*) along with other pictures of Arles including *Café de Nuit* and *Le Pont de Langlois*.

Not only is Arles a city of arts and an ancient historical and cultural crossroads, but it is also surrounded by beautiful, varied countryside, making it the perfect centre for exploring the arid plains of Crau, the jagged Alpille mountains, the fertile banks of the swiftly flowing Rhône, and the untamed land of the Camargue (▶ 17).

Arles' main square, the Place du Forum, often frequented by Van Gogh

A Walk Around Arles

Start in Place de la République.

Distance
2km

Time
1 hour/full day with visits

Start/end point
place de la République
⊞ 51B1

Once the centre of the Roman metropolis, this square is flanked by the cathedral (▶ 50), the Church of Sainte Anne and the Town Hall.

Leave the square up rue du Cloître past the Théâtre Antique (▶ 51). Go right into rue de la Calade, anticlockwise around the Arène (▶ 50) past Place de la Major, then turn right down rue Raspail.

Sunny place de la Major, with its tiny Romanesque church, affords sweeping views across the Crau plain to the Alpille hills and is scene of the famous fête des gardians on 1 May (▶ 60).

Cross rue 4 Septembre into rue de Grille towards the Rhône. Turn right along the river bank past Musée Reattu (entrance in rue du Grand Prieure) until you reach Place Constantin.

Musée Reattu, housed in a 15th-century priory, contains an intriguing set of 57 coloured sketches by Picasso.

Turn left up rue Dominique Maisto, past the Themes de Constantin, and straight on into rue de l'Hôtel de Ville. Turn right at rue due Arènes until you reach the place du Forum.

Arles has a wealth of decorative features such as this fountain

Place du Forum is the heart of Arles and a favourite meeting place for locals and tourists. Note the Corinthian columns embedded into the wall of the Hôtel Nord-Pinus (▶ 101).

Lunch
La Vaccarès (££)
✉ place du Forum (entrance at 9 rue Favorin)
☎ 04 90 96 06 17

Leave the square along rue du Palais then turn right into rue Balze past the Cryptoportiques (▶ 50). Bear left at rue Mistral then left into the busy pedestrian shopping street, rue de la République, past Muséon Arlaton (▶ 51) and back to place de la République.

49

Van Gogh stayed at the Espace Van Gogh, a local hospital, soon after he cut his ear off

What to See in Arles

LES ALYSCAMPS   ✪✪

Accordng to custom, the Roman necropolis of Alyscamps (Latin *Elisii Campi* -Elysian Fields) was built outside the city walls along the Via Aurelia. The Christians took over the cemetery and several miracles are said to have taken place here, including the appearance of Christ. Burial here was so sought after that the dead were sealed in barrels and floated down the Rhône to Arles with a piece of gold between their teeth for the gravedigger. Formerly the necropolis had 19 chapels and several thousand tombs. Today, all that remains is a tranquil poplar-lined alleyway lined with moss-covered tombs.

ARÈNE   ✪✪✪

Built during the 1st century, this was the largest amphitheatre in Gaul (136m long and 107m wide), able to seat over 20,000 spectators and scene of blood-thirsty contests between gladiators and wild animals. Originally three storeys high, each with 60 marble-clad arcades and an awning to protect the audience from the elements. During the Middle Ages the stones from the third level were used to build two churches and 200 houses inside the arena to shelter the poor. These were demolished in 1825, leaving the amphitheatre once again free for bullfights (► 48).

ÈGLISE ST TROPHIME   ✪✪

A masterpiece of Provençal Romanesque. The original church was built in the 5th century, then rebuilt at the end of the 11th century, and the ornate tympanum, depicting the Last Judgement, was added in the next century. By contrast, the austerity of the interior is striking. The cloisters of St-Trophime, with their rich carvings and sensitively-illuminated chapels hung with Aubusson tapestries, are among the treasures of Provence.

LES ALYSCAMPS
- 51C1
- ✉ avenue des Alyscamps
- 🕐 Apr–Sept, 9–7, Oct–Mar 10–4:30. Closed 1 Jan, 1 Nov, 25 Dec
- ℹ Arles Tourist Office: Esplanade Charles de Gaulle (☎ 04 90 18 41 20)
- ♿ Good
- 💷 Moderate

ARÈNE
- 51C2
- ✉ Rond-point des Arènes
- ☎ 04 90 49 36 36
- 🕐 Apr–Sept, 9–7, Oct–Mar 10–4:30. Closed 1 Jan, 1 Nov, 25 Dec and occasional days for bullfights
- ♿ Few
- 💷 Moderate
- ↔ Théâtre Antique (► 51)

ÈGLISE ST TROPHIME
- 52B2
- ✉ place de la République
- 🕐 Daily 10–4:15; Cloister: Apr–Sep, 9–7; Oct–Mar 10–4:30
- ♿ Few
- 💷 Cloister: moderate
- ↔ Théâtre Antique (► 51)

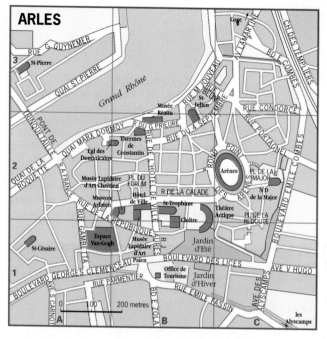

ARLES

ESPACE VAN GOGH ●●

It was in Arles that Vincent Van Gogh cut off his ear and gave it to a surprised prostitute! Arles was outraged, and was greatly relieved when he voluntarily entered the local hospital in 1889. Its garden has been restored to match the Dutch artist's descriptions.

🕂 51A1
✉ rue Président Wilson
☎ 04 90 49 39 39
🕐 Courtyard always open
♿ Good 🎟 Free

MUSÉE DE L'ARLES ANTIQUE ●●●

This splendid museum is an absolute must-see. It is built over the Cirque Romaine, an enormous 2nd century chariot racecourse, which is currently being excavated. It is a modern museum covering the history of the area from Roman rule to the Christian era.

🕂 51A2
✉ Presqu'île du Cirque Romain
☎ 04 90 18 88 89
🕐 10–6. Closed Tue, 1 Jan, 1 May, 25 Dec
♿ Excellent 🎟 Expensive

MUSÉON ARLATEN ●

Poet Frédéric Mistral founded the Muséon Arlaten in 1896, thus promoting a Provençal renaissance in Arles. It illustrates everyday life in the region, and includes a beautiful exhibition of Arlésien costume, still occasionally worn today.

🕂 51B2
✉ Hôtel Laval-Castellane, rue de la République
☎ 04 90 96 08 23
🕐 9–12, 2–5. Closed Mon
♿ None 🎟 Moderate

THÉÂTRE ANTIQUE ●

Sadly, fanatical Christians destroyed a large part of the Roman Antique Theatre (1 BC). Fragments lie forgotten among the bushes and the flowers, suggesting it was even more lavish than the theatre in Orange (▶ 26).

🕂 51B2
✉ rue de la Calade
☎ 04 90 96 93 30
🕐 9–7; Oct–Mar 10–4:.30
♿ None 🎟 Moderate

Aix-en-Provence

+ 28B2
ℹ Aix-en-Provence Tourist Office: place du Général de Gaulle (☎ 04 42 16 11 61)
↔ Luberon villages (➤ 38), Aubagne (➤ 56), Marseille (➤ 54)

One of Aix's many fountains

This old capital of Provence is splashed by nearly 100 fountains, a pleasing reminder that its very name comes from its waters, Aquae Sextiae, as the Romans named it in 123 BC. The city thrived culturally during the Middle Ages under Good King René, an ardent patron of the arts, reaching the height of its splendour during the 17th–18th centuries, with the construction of over 160 honey-hued hôtels particuliers (mansion-style residences) beautifully decorated with ornamental wrought-iron balconies.

What to see in Aix-en-Provence

+ 53B4
✉ 9 avenue Paul-Cézanne
☎ 04 42 21 05 78
🕐 Jun–Sep 10–12, 2:30–5:50; Oct–May 10–12, 2–5. Closed Tue and hols
♿ Few 🅿 Moderate
↔ Cathédrale St-Sauveur (➤ 52)

ATELIER CÉZANNE ✪✪
Paul Cézanne, Aix's most famous citizen, spent most of his life here painting the rugged limestone hills of the surrounding countryside (➤ 21). A special circuit *Cézanne* around town, marked by bronze pavement plaques, leads to the studio where he spent the last seven years of his life – poignantly just as he left it, with unfinished canvases, palettes and his old black hat.

+ 53B3

CATHÉDRALE ST-SAUVEUR ✪✪
Aix's main church combines a variety of architectural styles: the baptistry is 5th-century, the cloisters

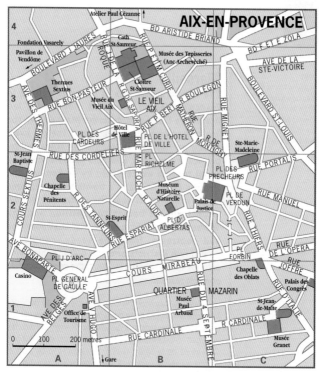

AIX-EN-PROVENCE

Romanesque, the transept and chancel Gothic and the main portal has magnificently carved walnut Renaissance doors. Don't miss Nicolas Froment's famous triptych *Le Buisson Ardent* (1475–6), depicting a vision of the Virgin and Child surrounded by the eternal burning bush of Moses.

☒ 24 place des Martyrs-de-la-Résistance
☎ 04 42 21 10 51
♿ Good
↔ Atelier Cézanne (➤ 52),

COURS MIRABEAU ✪✪✪

This mansion-lined avenue, named after the great revolutionary Comte de Mirabeau, and framed by a canopy of plane trees, plays centre stage to the wealthy Aixois society who promenade their poodles here between cups of coffee in *Les Deux Garçons*, and other Parisian-style cafés. The *cours* divides the town centre: The *Vieille Ville* (Old Town) to the north, and the Quartier Mazarin, with its fancy mansions, to the south.

✚ 53B1
☒ cours Mirabeau
ℹ Contact Aix Tourist Office for information
🍴 Pavement café
♿ Good
↔ Musée Granet (➤ 53)

MUSÉE GRANET ✪✪

The city's main museum, housed in the Gothic priory of the Knights of Malta, contains 19th-century Aixois artist François Granet's collection of French, Italian and Flemish paintings. A number of rooms are devoted to local artists, including eight canvases by Cézanne.

✚ 53C1
☒ place Saint-Jean-de-Malte
☎ 04 42 38 14 70
🕐 10–12, 2–6. Closed Tue in winter
♿ Few 💰 Expensive

53

28B1

Marseille Tourist Office:
4 La Canebière (☎ 04
91 54 91 11)

Metro 1 (Vieux Port)

Aix-en–Provence (► 52),
Aubagne (► 56), Cassis
(► 57)

Marseille

The extraordinary mix of race and culture in France's premier port and oldest city, led Alexandre Dumas to describe Marseille as the 'meeting place of the entire world'. The city has a strong personality, its reputation sustained by political corruption, sporadic gangsterism, and racial tension exacerbated by Le Pen and the National Front. It is also a traditional city, famous for its shipping, its soap, its Pastis, the world's largest annual boules competition and the 'Marseillaise' (► 55); a city full of contradictions and contrasts, from the seedy, congested downtown districts and the hideous high-rise suburbs to the vibrant old port, the sandy beaches and chic residences of the Corniche.

For an overview of the city, visit the Musée du Vieux Marseille and find time to see some of the many architectural gems: the recently discovered Roman Jardin des Vestiges, 5th-century Basilique St Victor, ostentatious Cathédrale de la Major (1893), the largest to be built in France for many centuries, and Corbusier's avant-garde *Cité Radieuse* (1952) (► 101).

Marseille is not an obvious tourist destination and it is admittedly not always easy to find the treasures which lie hidden in this frenetic and sprawling city, but visitors who take the trouble will be richly rewarded.

What to See in Marseille

28B1

rue Fort du Sanctuaire

Oct–May 7–7; Jun–Sep
7–8

60

Free

BASILIQUE DE NOTRE-DAME-DE-LA-GARDE   ✪✪

Marseille's major landmark, standing proudly 162m above the city, is a massive neo-Byzantine extravaganza topped by a gaudy golden Madonna. The views over the city are unforgettable, as are the model fishing boats and unusual votive offerings painted by fishermen and sailors inside the church.

28B1

7, 8, 31, 33, 34, 80, 81

LA CANEBIÈRE   ✪

Took its name from the Provençal *canébe* (cannabis), originally running from former hemp fields to the rope-making heart of the old port. Once considered the Champs Elysées of Marseille, lined with fancy shops, grand cafés and luxury hotels, it has since lost much of its former grandeur, but remains very much *the* place for shopping.

CHATEAU D'IF ✪✪

This forbidding fortress castle lies 3km offshore on the barren, rocky Île du Frioul. Its long history represents an extraordinary blend of fact, fiction and legend. Built in 1528 by François I to protect the port, it later became a prison, with famous inmates including the legendary Man in the Iron Mask and also Alexander Dumas' fictional Count of Monte Cristo.

✚ 28B1
☎ 04 91 59 02 30
◷ Daily 9–5. Closed 1 Jan, 25 Dec, Mon in school hols
🍴 Bar-Restaurant (££)
🛥 Quai des Belges (☎ 04 91 55 50 09)
♿ Few 🎧 Moderate

PALAIS LONGCHAMP – MUSÉE DES BEAUX ARTS ✪✪

This grandiose 1860s palace houses Marseille's main art gallery, packed with masterpieces by Rubens, Brueghel, Corot and local Marseille artists.

✚ 28B1
✉ Palais Longchamp, 4e
☎ 04 91 62 21 17
◷ Summer 11–6; winter 10–5. Closed Mon
Ⓜ Metro 1 (Longchamp–Cinq-Avenues)
♿ Good
🎧 Moderate

> ### Did you know ?
>
> *During the French Revolution, 500 volunteers were sent from Marseille to Paris. As they marched northwards, they sang a song, recently composed by Rouget de Lisle in Strasbourg. By the time they reached Paris, it had been adopted as the anthem of the revolution, and was named La Marseillaise in honour of the city's 'choir'.*

Colourful fishing boats clutter the old port

† 28A2

ℹ Les Baux-de-Provence
Tourist Office: Ilot 'Post
Tenebras Lux' (☎ 04 90
54 34 39)

↔ Arles (➤ 48), St-Rémy-
de-Provence (➤ 58)

**Les-Baux-de-Provence
Citadelle**

✉ Ville Morte

☎ 04 90 54 55 56

🕐 Mar–Nov 8–7:30; Jul–Aug
8–9; Nov–Feb 9–5:30

💷 Very expensive

**Musée des Amis du Vieil
Eygalières**

✉ Chapelle des Pénitents

☎ 04 90 95 91 52

🕐 Apr–Oct, Sun 3–6

♿ Few

💷 Free

† 29C1

ℹ Aubagne Tourist Office:
avenue Antide Boyer
(☎ 04 42 03 49 98)

↔ Marseille (➤ 54–5),
Cassis (➤ 57)

What to See in Bouches-du-Rhône

LES ALPILLES

South of St-Rémy-de-Provence lies a thirsty landscape of crumpled white limestone crags – the Chaine des Alpilles. Market gardens, vineyards and long avenues of plane-trees on the lower slopes give way to olive groves and scrub, splashed with yellow broom, lilac lavender and scented wild thyme. This area is easy to explore on foot, horseback or bike, and you are unlikely to meet anyone except the occasional flock of sheep!

Often called 'the Pompeii of Provence', the ancient ruined citadel of Les-Baux-de-Provence clings to one of the highest ridges of the Alpilles. Lex Baux is divided into two: the bustling inhabited lower village, where elegant Renaissance houses line the shiny cobbled streets, and the deserted Ville Morte perched above, its ruined buildings hardly distinguishable from the surrounding milky-white limestone crags.

During the Middle Ages, this was the seat of the seigneurs de Baux, one of Southern France's most powerful families. Their Cour d'Amour – a dazzling society of lords, ladies and wandering troubadours – was renowned throughout the Midi and, ever since, Les Baux has been a romantic pilgrimage centre for poets and painters.

Picturesque Eygalières is hidden off the beaten track, surrounded by a wild, dusty landscape of olive and cypress trees. Its creamy stone houses, with sky blue and aquamarine shutters, line the lanes leading up to the village chapel (which now houses the village museum), a ruined castle and a spectacular panorama of the Alpilles. Try to visit during the first weekend of August, when this sleepy village hosts a merry fête and a splendid torchlit Arlésienne horseback parade.

AUBAGNE

This old market town is now virtually a suburb of Marseille and yet, thanks to its thriving craft traditions, it has largely preserved its individual charm. Aubagne is well known for its pottery (particularly the small earthenware figures called *santons* which originated here) and as the birthplace of the writer, Marcel Pagnol. Recent films of his famous novels *Jean de Florette* and *Manon des Sources* have brought him to new prominence and admirers of his work can visit such sights as Manon's fountain and Pagnol's grave at La Treille by following clearly signed tours into the wild countryside that surrounds the town.

CASSIS ✪✪

This cheerful little fishing port and beach resort basks in a sheltered bay between the cliffs of the Cap Canaille, Europe's highest sea cliffs, and the breathtaking *calanques* to the west (►16). The surrounding hills are smothered with olives, almonds, figs, and the famous terraced vineyards of the region's highly-reputed white wine. In the village centre, *boccia* players meet in dusty squares while fishermen spread their nets along the bustling quayside, beside its colourful waterfront cafés. To explore the wondrous coastline, take a boat trip from a landing stage on the quay.

➕ 28B1
ℹ Cassis Tourist Office: place Baragnon (☎ 04 42 01 71 17)
↔ Marseille (►54), Aubagne (►56)

STE-MARIES-DE-LA-MER ✪✪✪

The picture-postcard fishing village of Ste Maries-de-la-Mer is steeped in the tradition and folklore of the Camargue (►17) with its ancient white-washed cottages, colourful costumes, bloodthirsty bull-fights and flame-red sunsets. According to legend, the Virgin Mary's half-sisters Maria Jacobé and Maria Salome landed here in AD 40 with their black serving-maid Sarah, patroness of gypsies. When they died a chapel was built over their graves (later replaced by Notre-Dame-de-la-Mer) and the village has been a place of pilgrimage ever since.

The main pilgrimage takes place on 24–5 May. Gypsies, dressed in flounced skirts, brilliant shawls, ribbons and flowers, carry statues of the Marias and the bejewelled black Sarah in a small blue boat into the sea to be blessed, led by handsome mounted *gardiens* in full Camargue cowboy dress. There then follows a sparkling festival of bullfighting, rodeos, flamenco and fireworks.

➕ 28A1
✉ Ste-Marie-de-la-Mer Tourist Office: 5 avenue Van Gogh (☎ 04 90 97 82 55)
↔ Arles (►48)

A boat trip from Cassis is the best way to see the cliffs and coastline

57

🕂 28B2

ℹ️ Rémy-de-Provence
Tourist Office (☎ 04 90
92 05 22)

↔️ Avignon (➤ 31), Cavaillon
(➤ 41), Les-Baux-de-
Provence (➤ 56), Les
Alpilles villages (➤ 56,
59), Tarascon (➤ 58)

Glanum

☎ 04 90 92 23 79

🕐 Apr–Sep, daily 9–7;
Oct–Mar 9–12, 2–5.
Closed 1 Jan, 1 May, 11
Nov, 25 Dec

♿ None

💷 Expensive

❓ Plan showing a
reconstruction of the site
available at entrance

🕂 28A2

ℹ️ Tarascon Tourist Office
(☎ 04 90 91 03 52)

↔️ Avignon (➤ 31); Arles
(➤ 48), Les Alpilles
(➤ 56, 59), St Rémy-de-
Provence (➤ 58)

Château de Tarascon

✉️ boulevard de Roi René

☎ 04 90 91 01 93

🕐 Oct–Mar, daily Mon–Fri
9–12, 2–5; Apr–Sep, daily
9–7. Closed 1 Jan, 1
May, 1 and 11 Nov, 25
Dec

♿ Few 💷 Moderate

❓ Guided tours by
reservation only

*Rust-coloured rooftops,
viewed from Good King
Rene's fortress*

58

ST-RÉMY-DE-PROVENCE ✪✪

Here you will find the true flavour of Provence – the warm peaches-and-cream coloured buildings, the maze of lanes, the fountains, the squares and the tree-lined boulevards. Nostradamus was born here in 1503, but today St-Rémy owes its popularity to Van Gogh, who convalesced in an asylum just south of town after his quarrel with Gauguin and the ear-cutting incident in Arles. He produced 150 canvases and over 100 drawings during his one year's stay here, including Starry Night, The Sower and his famous Irises.

Near the asylum lie the extensive remains of the wealthy Greco-Roman town of **Glanum**, the oldest civilised buildings in France. The area, covering about 2 hectares (5 acres), was first settled in 6 BC and that the city but abandoned in the 3rd century when it was overrun by Barbarians. Buildings nearby, called *Les Antiques*, were also part of the Roman town: the oldest and smallest triumphal arch in France, dating from 20 BC and the best-preserved mausoleum of the Roman world, erected as a memorial to Caesar and Augustus.

TARASCON ✪

Most people visit Tarascon, former frontier town of the kingdom of Provence, to visit the Renaissance **fortress** of Good King René, with its moat and turreted towers on the banks of the Rhône. The town is also famous for its dreaded Tarasque, a man-eating monster who, according to legend, was vanquished by the town's patron Sainte Marthe. On the last Sunday in June the green, dragon-like papier-maché Tarasque parades around town, accompanied by Tartarin, a colourful character created by Alphonse Daudet, who mocks the *petite bourgeoisie* of Provence. This starts four days of fun for all the family – festivities, fireworks, bonfires and bullfights.

A Drive from Arles Round The Alpilles to Tarascon

Head north-west out of Arles along the N570 then the D17 to the Abbey of Montmajour.

Once surrounded by marshes, this former Benedictine abbey is considered one of the most elaborate Romanesque churches in Provence.

Take the next turning right (D82), then over a crossroads, following signs to 'Aqueduc Romain'.

These two ruined aquaducts once conveyed water from the Alpilles to Arles.

Back at the crossroads, turn right past the old windmill that inspired 19th-century novelist Alphonse Daudet to write his masterwork Lettres de mon Moulin *at Fontvieille. Leave town on the D17 through Paradou and continue to Maussane-les-Alpilles.*

Taste the wines of 14th-century Château d'Estoublon Mogador just outside Fontvieille, or buy their prize-winning olive oil.

Once through Maussane, fork left on to the D78 following signs to Le Destet and Eygalières (▶ 56). Exit Eygalières on the D74A. Turn left at the main road to St-Rémy-de-Provence (▶ 58). From here, take a small, unsignposted lane out of place de la République to St Etienne-de-Grès.

Hometown of the Provencal fabric manufacturer Olivades. Visit their factory here.

Continue on the D32 towards Arles to reach a busy junction beside a church.

Only the church remains of the Gallo-Roman port of St Gabriel, with one of the finest Romanesque façades in the Midi. The port flourished until the Middle Ages when the canal dried up.

Turn right at the junction, then take the D970 at the roundabout into Tarascon (▶ 58).

Distance
85 km

Time
3 ¼ hours without stops; full day with visits

Remains of the roman aquaducts which once supplied water to Arles

Start point
Arles
✚ 28A2

End point
Tarascon
✚ 28A2

Lunch
Café des Arts, St-Rémy-de-Provence
✉ 30 boulevard Victor Hugo
☎ 04 90 92 08 50

In the Know

If you only have a short time to visit Provence and the Côte d'Azur, or would like to get a real flavour of the region, here are some ideas:

10 Ways To Be A Local

While away the hours in the local village bar.
Develop a taste for *Pastis*.
Try your hand at *pétanque*.
Take a siesta.
Chat to locals about culinary delights, sport and politics.
Remember to address people as *monsieur*, *madame* or *mademoiselle*.
Sunbathe topless (but don't walk around town in beachwear afterwards)!
Relish the local cuisine.
Shop in local markets and sample the food before you buy.

Relax, unwind and settle into the provençal pace of life.

10 Top Events

Aix International Festival of Music and Lyric Arts (Jul) – France's most élite music festival.
Arles *Gardian* Festival (Apr) – Camarguais cowboys, *Arlésienne* girls, *farandole* dancing and bull-fights.
Avignon International Theatre Festival (Jul–Aug) – mainstream and fringe theatre.
Cannes International Film Festival (May, ► 116, 85).

Châteauneuf-du-Pape Grape Ripening Festival (Aug) – troubadours, jousting, jugglers, banquets and free wine-tasting.
Dignes Lavender Festival (Aug) – Provence's most sweet smelling festival.
Menton Lemon Festival (Feb) – spectacular procession of floats made out of 130 tonnes of golden citrus fruit.
Monaco Grand Prix (May) – Formula One in the streets of Monte Carlo.
Nice Carnival (Feb) – the Riviera's biggest winter event.
Nice Jazz Festival (July) – Europe's leading open-air jazz festival, in an olive grove.

10 Top Activities

Take a helicopter from Nice Airport to Monte Carlo (Héli Inter Riviera ☎ 04 93 21 46 46).
Go fishing and cook your catch on board (Sea Cruises Golfe-Juan ☎ 93 42 08 45).
Visit the Îles de Lérins (Compagnie Maritime Cannoise ☎ 04 93 38 66 33).
Hang-glide off the top of Mont Ventoux (Ciel Mont Ventoux ☎ 04 90 65 13 11).

An elaborate display at Menton's Lemon Festival

Rehearsing for the bullfight

Take a boat trip to Corsica from Nice's old port (SNCM ☎ 04 93 13 66 66).

Ski Serre-Chevalier, Provence's largest ski resort (☎ 04 92 21 08 50).

Hire a Harley Davidson and cruise the streets of St Tropez (St Tropez Cars ☎ 04 94 97 10 34).

Take the 'Pinecone Train' from Nice to Dignes-les-Bains (☎ 04 93 82 10 17).

Canoe the Grand Canyon du Verdon (Verdon Insolite, ☎ 04 92 77 33 57).

Spend a weekend with wine-makers, cherry- or olive-picking, or truffle-hunting (Voyages Arnaud ☎ 04 90 60 43 33).

5
Top Beaches

Cannes – best for star-spotting.
Cassis, (Calanques) – most scenic (▶16).
Iles d'Hyères (Plage de la Palud, Port-Cros) – best island beach.
Marseille (Plage du Prophète) – best watersports.
St Tropez (La Voile Rouge) – the trendiest (▶66).

5
Top Gardens

Cap Férat – Villa Ephrussi de Rothschild.
Monaco – Jardin Exotic.
Nice – Phoenix Parc Floral.
Entrecasteaux – château gardens.
Sérignan-du-Comtat – botanical herb garden.

Boating on the Grand Canyon du Verdon

5
Top Markets

Aix-en-Provence (Flower Market – Tue, Thu, Sat am) – all the fragrance and colour of Provence.
Arles (Sat am Market) – an opportunity to see the Arlésienne women in traditional dress. Fruit, vegetables, soaps and fabrics, also saddles and stirrups.
Aubagne (Argilla) – biennial pottery market – the largest in France.
Marseille (Fish Market) – ad hoc boatside stalls.
Nice (cours Saleya) – voted one of France's most exceptional markets.

Var & Haute-Provence

No region of Provence displays such great diversity as the Var, the Alpes-de-Haute-Provence and the Hautes-Alpes. The Var boasts Provence's longest coastal strip, wild and rugged with deserted creeks and bleached beaches, far less developed than its famous Riviera neighbour. Its resorts are strung out like pearls along the coast, with St Tropez the jewel in the crown. Inland, the Var is the most wooded district of France, with sombre green forests of chestnuts, cork-oaks and conifers, interrupted only by an occasional yellow splash of mimosa or a quaint, hidden village.

By contrast, the two mountainous *départements* of Haute-Provence boast some of Provence's most sensational scenery, including Europe's 'Grand Canyon', the Gorges du Verdon. Picturebook villages and towns, rich in Provençal and Alpine architecture, bear witness to an eventful past, while the bracing mountain air embraces all the intoxicating perfumes of Provence.

— ❦ —

*' If you would like to see
the most beautiful land in
the world, here it is '*

PIERRE AUGUST RENOIR
(in a letter to Berthe Morisot)

———— • ————

69C1

St Tropez

Even though the hedonistic image of St Tropez in the Swinging Sixties has grown distinctly jaded, this charming little fishing port continues to seduce visitors and, despite being a tourist honeypot, remains a magnet for the rich and famous. In the words of the French writer Colette: 'Once you have visited here, you will never want to leave.'

Most visitors come to St Tropez to rub shoulders with the glitterati in the waterfront cafés, and admire the grandiose yachts, moored before a backdrop of pink and yellow pastel-hued buildings. These are relatively modern, but were reconstructed following the original designs after the destruction which occurred during World War II. But take time to explore the narrow streets and medieval squares of old St Tropez, where you will find a village of great character with its colourful markets, chic boutiques and romantic bistros.

Rub shoulders with the rich and famous at Le Gorille – always an 'in' bar

Founded by Greeks as Athenopolis (City of Athena), the town has long been a popular meeting place for artists. Liszt and Maupassant were its first celebrities in the 1880s, followed by neo-Impressionist painter Signac a decade later. Soon Matisse, Bonnard, Utrillo and Dufy fell under St Tropez' spell, immortalising the town in paint. Many pictures can be seen in the Musée de L'Annonciade (► 67).

Between the wars arrived an influx of writers, including Colette, Cocteau and Anaïs Nin. Then in the 1950s it was the turn of the film stars, led by the famous Tropézienne, Brigit Bardot. Her scandalous film, *Et Dieu Créa La Femme (And Woman Was Created)* of 1956, marked the start of a new, permissive era and the Bardot/St Tropez cult.

St Tropez' star-studded list of residents includes Elton John, George Michael, Jean-Paul Belmondo and Jean Michel Jarre and, although it may no longer be how it was in its heyday, everything here is still extravagant, decadent, excessive. Little wonder the French endearingly call it St 'Trop' (literally. 'too much').

A Walk Around St Tropez

Start on the waterfront. Beside the Tourist Office, go through the Porte de la Poissonnerie, past the marble slabs of the daily fish market into place aux Herbes.

A stone's throw from the glitz and glamour of the quayside, the colourful daily fish, fruit and vegetable stalls remind visitors of St Tropez' modest village past.

Leave the square up the steps of rue du Marché, turn left into rue des Commerçants, first right into rue du Clocher to the Eglise St Tropez (➤ 66). Continue along rue Cdt Guichard to place de la Mairie, dominated by its handsome pink and green town hall, and place Garrezio.

The massive tower here is all that remains of St Tropez' oldest building, 10th-century Château de Suffren, once home of the great 18th-century seaman, Admiral Suffren.

Return past the town hall and along rue de la Ponche. The 15th-century Porche de la Ponche archways lead to the old Ponche quarter.

This is the old fishing district of St Tropez, centred on the sun-baked Place du Revelin, overlooking the unspoilt fishing port and tiny pebble beach.

Head up rue des Ramparts, right at rue d'Aumale to the delightful place de l'Ormeau, and left up rue de l'Ormeau to rue de la Citadelle. Proceed downhill towards the port, taking the first left into rue Portail Neuf as far as the chapel.

The Chapelle de la Miséricorde with its quaint bell tower dates from the 17th century and the road alongside passes through its flying buttresses. The chapel's entrance is on rue Gambetta.

Continue along rue Gambetta for lunch in Place des Lices (➤ 67).

Distance
1½km

Time
1–1 ½ hours, depending on church visits.

Start point
Waterfront
✚ 69C1

End point
Place des Lices
✚ 69C1

Lunch
Café des Arts (£)
✉ Place des Lices
☎ 04 94 97 02 25

It's not all gin-palaces and multi-millionaire's yachts at St Tropez

What to See in St Tropez

LA CITADELLE ⭐⭐

Visit this 16th-century hilltop fortress if only for the view, which embraces the orange curly-tiled roofs of St Tropez' *vieille ville*, the dark and distant Maures and Esterel hills, and the glittering blue of the bay, flecked with sails. The Citadel contains a naval museum, illustrating the town's long and glorious history, right up to the 1944 Allied landings which destroyed so much of the town.

✚ 69C1
✉ Montée de la Citadelle
☎ 04 94 97 59 43
🕐 Mid-Jun to mid-Sep 10–6; winter 10–5. Closed Tue
♿ Few
👆 Very expensive

EGLISE DE ST TROPEZ ⭐

St Tropez owes its name to a Roman centurion called Torpes, who was martyred under Nero in AD 68. His head was buried in Pisa and his body put in a boat with a dog and cockerel who were to devour it. However, when the boat washed up here, his remains were miraculously untouched. For over 400 years, the town's most important festival – the Bravade de Saint-Tropez (► 116) – has been celebrated in his honour. You can see a gilt bust of St Torpes and a model of his boat in the 19th-century baroque-style church, with its distinctive pink and yellow bell-tower.

✚ 69C1
✉ rue de l'Église
🕐 Daily
↔ Viex Port (► 67)

Tourist Office
ℹ quai Jean Jaurès
☎ 04 94 97 45 21
↔ Cogolin (► 69), Port Grimaud (► 71)

St Tropez Beaches
Le Club 55
✉ boulevard Patch
☎ 04 94 79 80 14

Tahiti Plage
✉ route de Tahiti
☎ 04 94 97 18 02

La Voile Rouge
✉ route des Tamaris
☎ 04 94 97 84 34

> ### Did you know ?
>
> It was at the gorgeous sandy beaches of surrounding St Tropez that girls first dared to bathe topless in the 1960s. In total, there are over 6kms of enticing golden sand, neatly divided into invididual beaches, each with a different character, including trendy Club 55, which caters for the Paris set. Plage de Tahiti was once the movie stars' favourite, but nowadays star-spotters have more luck at the frivolous La Voile Rouge.

MUSÉE DE L'ANNONCIADE ✪✪✪

This former 16th-century chapel houses one of the finest collections of French late 19th-and early 20th-century paintings and bronzes. St Tropez was then one of the most active centres of the artistic avant-garde and, as a result, most of the 100 or so canvases here belong to the great turn-of-the-century movements of pointillism, fauvism and nabism. Many of the paintings portray local scenes. Look for Paul Signac's *L'Orage* (1895), Bonnard's *Le Port de St Tropez* (1899), Camoin's *La Place des Lices* (1925), works by Dufy, Derain, Vuillard and others – and the museum cat, called Matisse!

> ⊞ 69C1
> ✉ place Georges Grammont
> ☎ 04 94 97 04 01
> 🕐 Jun–Sep, 10–12, 3–7; Oct–May, 10–12, 2–6. Closed Tue, 1 Jan, 1 May, Ascension, Nov, 25 Dec
> ♿ Few
> 💲 Expensive
> ↔ Vieux Port (►67)

PLACE DES LICES ✪✪

This is the real heart of St Tropez, and remains very much as it looked in Camoin's *La Place des Lices* of 1925 (► above), lined with ancient plane trees and bohemian cafés. The best time to visit is on Tuesdays or Saturdays for its colourful market, but come anytime for a game of *boules* and a glass of *pastis* with the locals.

> ⊞ 69C1
> ✉ place des Lices
> 🍽 Café des Arts (►65)
> ♿ Good
> ❓ Shuttle buses to the beaches of Pampelonne (►66) in summer

VIEUX PORT ✪✪✪

Artists and writers have been enticed to the pretty pastel-painted houses and crowded cafés which line the quay for over a century. Today, the waterfront is very much the place to see and be seen in St Tropez, so try to arrive in your Aston Martin, on your Harley Davidson, or better still in an enormous floating gin palace, and remember to moor stern-to, giving onlookers a good view! It's such fun to wander along the quayside, to marvel at the size and cost of these ostentatious yachts, and to watch their millionaire owners tucking into langoustines on deck, flamboyantly served by white-frocked crew.

> ⊞ 69C1
> ✉ Vieux Port
> 🍽 Harbourfront bars, cafés and restaurants include Sénéquier's (►97)
> ♿ Good
> ❓ Musée de l'Annonciade (►67)

Two places to be seen – the beach; the pastel-coloured waterfront

67

What to See in Var

AUPS ✪✪

69B2

Aups Tourist Office:
place Frédéric Mistral
(☎ 04 94 70 00 80)

Grand Canyon du Verdon
(► 20), Moustiers-Ste-
Marie (► 74)

The peaceful walled village of Aups basks in a wide valley, backed by undulating hills smothered in vines and olives, its name deriving from the Celto-Ligurian *alb* (hill pasture). The village enjoys a local reputation for its wine, honey, oil, black truffles and other regional specialities sold at the local Thursday-morning market. With its friendly folk, medieval gateways, shady streets, small squares dotted with fountains and a charming little museum of modern art in an old converted convent, Aups offers the perfect getaway from the well-trodden tourist tracks of Provence.

BORMES-LES-MIMOSAS ✪✪

69B1

Bormes-Les-Mimosas
Tourist Office: 9
place Gambetta
(☎ 04 94 71 15 17)

Collobrières (► 70)

Despite a chequered history – founded by the Gauls, conquered by the Romans, then continually sacked by Saracens, Corsairs, Moors, Genoese and finally during the Wars of Religion – this hillside village remains one of the prettiest villages of the entire coast. Its ice-cream coloured pantiled houses spiral down steep stairways and alleys, with amusing names – Lover's Lane (Venelle des Amoreux), Gossipers Way (Draille des Bredovilles) and steepest of all, Bottom-Breaker Road (Roumpi-Cuou)! Depending on the season, Bormes is bathed in the scent of mimosa, eucalyptus, oleander and camomile. In February, when the mimosa is in full bloom, it celebrates with its sensational *corso fleuri* – an extravaganza of floral floats made from myriads of tiny yellow flowers.

A *circuit touristique* embraces most of the sights including a fine 16th-century chapel dedicated to patron Saint François-de-Paule, an 18th-century church built in Romanesque style, a museum of local art, countless craft shops and a ruined castle, affording dazzling seaward views to the Îles d'Or (P71) and inland over the Massif des Maures (P70).

The circuit touristique *is a riot of flowers throughout the year*

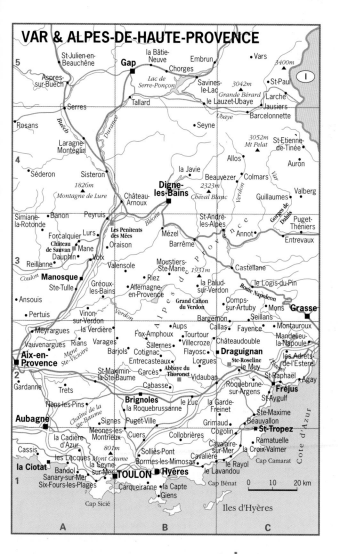

VAR & ALPES-DE-HAUTE-PROVENCE

COGOLIN ⭐

Old Cogolin, with its brightly coloured medieval houses, narrow cobbled streets and peaceful hidden *placettes* (tiny squares) bursting with flowers, offers a welcome escape from the crowds of nearby St Tropez. Cogolin's economy depends on the traditional crafts of making cane furniture, silk yarn, brier pipes, knotted wool carpets and above all, reeds for wind instruments, attracting musicians of international renown.

✚ 69C1

ℹ Cogolin Tourist Office: place de la République (☎ 04 94 54 63 17) – also organises visits to craft factories

↔ St Tropez (►64), Port-Grimaud (►71)

69B1

Collobrières Tourist Office: boulevard Charles-Caminat (☎ 04 94 48 08 00)

Bormes-les-Mimosas (►68)

69C2

Cannes (►85), Fréjus (►70)

69C2

Fréjus Tourist Office: 325 rue Jean Jaurès (☎ 04 94 17 19 19)

St Tropez (►64), Cannes (►85)

Arène Fréjus

☎ 04 94 17 05 60

Apr–Sep, 9:30–11:45, 2–8; Oct–Mar, 9–11:45, 2–4:15. Closed Tue

Moderate

COLLOBRIÈRES ✪✪

The tranquil village of Collobrières lies alongside the River Collobrier at the heart of the wild Massif des Maures, surrounded by densely forested hillside of cork-oaks and chestnut trees bearing fruits the size of tennis balls. Collobrières is reputed to have been first in France to learn about corkage from the Spanish in the Middle Ages and cork production is still the major industry in the village, together with *marrons glacés* and other sweet chestnut confectionery.

CORNICHE D'OR ✪✪✪

In stark contrast to the over-developed resorts to the east, the 'golden' Esterel Coast remains the sole stretch of wild coast left between St Raphaël and the Italian border: a ragged shoreline of startlingly red cliffs, tumbling into a bright blue sea from the craggy wilderness of the Massif de l'Esterel beyond, piercing the coast with minute inlets, secret coves and tiny deserted bays. A narrow road (N98) twists along the clifftop, dipping down through some of the coast's least pretentious resorts, including Miramar and Agay. Inland, the blood-red porphyry mountains of the *Massif*, for centuries the haunt of bandits, are smothered in brilliant green spruce, pine and scrub, and ignited by wild flowers in summer.

FRÉJUS ✪

The oldest Roman city in Gaul, founded by Julius Caesar in 49 BC, the flourishing naval town of Fréjus (*Forum Julii*) lay on the Aurelian Way from Rome to Arles. The fragile 1st- to 2nd-century **Roman arena** and theatre are still used for bullfights and concerts, and the remarkable Provençal cathedral contains one of France's oldest baptistries, perfectly-preserved and dating from the 4th or 5th century. Following the decline of the Roman Empire, the port lost its significance and eventually silted up, forming the sandy beaches of Fréjus-Plage, a modern resort which merges into St Raphaël.

Did you know ?

Ever since the Romans used it to scent their baths, lavender (from the Latin lavare *'to wash') has been in demand for its sweet smell and soothing qualities. There are two main types of plant: wild mountain lavender, which produces the most precious essences sought after by the makers of great perfumes, and* lavendin, *a hybrid grown in lower plains, which yields great quantities of inferior essence used in soap and other such products.*

GRIMAUD ⭐⭐

One of Provence's most photogenic *villages perchés*, Grimaud is crowned by a romantic 11th-century château belonging to the Grimaldi family, after whom the village is named. By contrast, the recently-created Port-Grimaud on the coast – a modern mini-Venice of ice cream-coloured designer villas lining the quayside designed by François Spoerry in the 1960s – is best viewed by water-taxi (*coche d'eau*) or from the church tower.

🚩 69C2
ℹ️ Port Grimaud
Information: 1 boulevard des Alziers, Grimaud
(☎ 04 94 43 36 98)
🍽️ Moderate
🔄 St Tropez (► 64), Cogolin (► 69)
❓ Tourist train links Port-Grimaud to the old hilltop village of Grimaud

Waterside mansions of Port Grimaud, Provence's mini-Venice; below, Hyères

HYÈRES ⭐

The oldest of the Côte d'Azur winter resorts, Hyères-les-Palmiers is so-called because of its important palm-growing industry. Its popularity in the early 19th century faded towards the end of the century due to it being 4km away from the newly-fashionable seaside. Hyères' main attraction today lies not in the town, but 10km off the Var coast – the three beautiful islands of the Îles d'Hyères.

🚩 69B1
ℹ️ Hyères Tourist Office: avenue de Belgique
(☎ 04 94 65 18 55)
⛴️ Five sailings daily for the Îles d'Or from Port de la Tour-Fondue, Presqu'île de Giens (☎ 04 94 58 21 81)

69C4

Colmars-Les-Alpes
Tourist Office: Porte de
Savoie (☎ 04 92 83 41
92)

Entrevaux (► 72)

Fort de Savoie

Summer: 2–6:30

Few

Expensive

69B4

Dignes-Les-Bains Tourist
Office: rond point du 11
Novembre 1918 (☎ 04
92 31 42 73)

Four trains a day

☎ 04 93 82 10 17 for times

Les Mées (► 74),
Sisteron (► 75)

Expensive

69C3

Entrevaux Tourist Office:
Porte Royale (☎ 04 93
05 46 73)

Colmars-les-Alpes (► 72)

Tourist office open
summer only. Guided
visits to Citadel in Jul and
Aug, 9–12, 3–6

What to See in Alpes-de-Haute-Provence

COLMARS-LES-ALPES   ✪

The name 'Colmars' stems from Roman times when a temple to the god Mars was erected on the hill (*Collis Martis*), which today forms the backdrop to this small fortified village. Hidden in a high wooded valley of the Haut-Verdon, amidst the highest peaks of the Alpes-de-Haute-Provence, the wooden alpine chalets, with their sloping roofs and balconies encrimsoned with geraniums, seem far removed from the stone *mas* of the Var. It is here that the kingdom of France once bordered Savoy, hence the impregnable ramparts and two massive medieval castles which crown the village, guarding the bridges at each end of the village. The northern Fort de Savoie, is the more imposing and contains a cultural centre where exhibtions are held in the summer.

DIGNES-LES-BAINS   ✪✪

This genteel town and departmental capital in the pre-Alps beside the River Bléone, lies on the Route Napoléon, used by the Emperor after his escape from Elba. Its sheltered location, mild sunny climate, invigorating air and the thermal springs to the south of town have made it a renowned spa centre.

Its other major attraction is lavender. This aromatic plant has been renowned since medieval times for its therapeutic qualities, and Digne is the lavender-growing capital of Provence. During the spectacular purple processions of the annual lavender festival (► 60), even the streets get doused with lavender water! There is a Route de la Lavande, which passes through Dignes and takes in all the main lavender producing places in the area. Dignes also marks the end of the 'Pinecone' line, an ancient train which runs through the beautiful mountain valleys to Nice four times a day.

ENTREVAUX   ✪✪

Sleepy Entrevaux was once an important border defence between France and Savoy, heavily fortified in the 1690s by Vauban, Louis XIV's military architect. Enter the village across a drawbridge, through one of three gatehouses into a hotchpotch of typically Provençal medieval houses, surprisingly untouched by the proximity of the Alps. The steep zig-zagging path to the mighty citadel which tops the ensemble is well worth the climb for the views of the Haut-Var and the encircling mountains beyond.

The picture-postcard village of Entrevaux

FORCALQUIER ✪

This old market town is situated on the Roman *Via Domita*, which linked the Alps with the Rhône delta. It takes its name from the limestone kilns (*furni calcarii*) which the Romans hewed into the hillside. During medieval times it was a powerful town and seat of the counts of Provence. Count Raimond, famous for his revelry, managed to marry off his four daughters to kings. On one occasion all four kings visited Forcalquier simultaneously and the region was dubbed the 'land of the four queens'! The surroundin-countryside is particularly lush and beautiful. According to the nearby **Observatory of Haute Provence**, it has the cleanest, clearest air of anywhere in France, and makes a good base to explore the *villages perchés* of Limans, Banon, Dauphin and Simiane-la-Rotonde.

GRAND CANYON DU VERDON (▶ 20, TOP TEN)

GRÉOUX-LES-BAINS ✪

Europe's oldest spa town lies in a beautiful, lavender and thyme-scented valley above the Verdon river, making it a perfect excursion base for outdoor sports, especially walking, cycling and fishing. Try its warm sulphurous waters, used since Roman times, and still popular today for treating arthritis, rheumatism and respiratory problems.

✚ 69A3
✉ 8 place Bourguet
☎ 04 92 75 10 02
↔ Les Mées (▶ 74), Sisteron (▶ 75)

Observatoire de Haute Provence
✉ St Michel
☎ 04 92 70 64 00
🕐 Apr–Sep, Wed 2–4 & 1st Sun of month 9–11
♿ Good
🚫 Expensive
❓ Guided tours only

✚ 69A3
✉ 5 avenue des Marronniers
☎ 04 92 78 01 08
↔ Forcalquier (▶ 73)

ℹ Moustiers-Ste-Marie
Tourist Office: Syndicat
d'Initiative (mid Jun–mid
Sep); Town Hall (rest of
year) (☎ 04 92 74 67
84/04 92 74 66 19)
↔ Grand Canyon du Verdon
(▶ 20), Aups (▶ 68)

MOUSTIERS-STE-MARIE ✪✪

Dramatically perched high on a ridge surrounded by sheer
cliffs, Moustiers marks the start of the great gorges of the
River Verdon (▶ 20). In the 17th and 18th centuries, its
white decorated earthenware pottery was famous
throughout the world. Now *Faïence de Moustiers* has
been revived and is sold in countless craft shops in every
cobbled square.

The 5th-century chapel of Notre Dame de Beauvour is
pinned against the rockface at the top of the village. Above
it hangs a renowned gold star, suspended on a 227-m
chain, presented to the village by a knight called Blacas to
celebrate his release from captivity during the Crusades.

✚ 69B3
ℹ Information: Château
Arnoux (☎ 04 92 64 02
64)
↔ Dignes-les-Bains (▶ 72),
Sisteron (▶ 75)

LES PENITENTS DES MÉES ✪

An extraordinary feature marks the entry into the Durance
valley from Digne and the Provençal Alps – curiously
eroded limestone pinnacles which stand tightly packed
together and towering 150m above the village of Les Mées
(named after the Latin *metae* or 'milestone'). According to a
5th-century legend, local monks were attracted to some
beautiful Moorish girls, captured by a knight during the
Saracen invasions. Disgraced, they were banished from the
village and, in punishment, turned to stone!

*The best buy in Moustiers
is undoubtedly its famous
white* Faïence *pottery*

What to See in Haute-Alpes

BRIANÇON ✪✪
This fortified city stands proudly amidst the lofty snow-capped mountain peaks of the southern Alps, and combines a rich historical past with an easy-going Provençal lifestyle. In summer, the surrounding countryside is a hikers' paradise, and in winter, Serres-Chevalier, one of France's top ski resorts, provides 250km of challenging ski slopes (▶ panel 110).

🚹 Off map
🛈 Briançon Tourist Office: Maison de Templiers (☎ 0492 21 01 01)

EMBRUN ✪
Gateway to the wilderness of the Queyras and the lofty peaks of the Ecrins mountains, this colourful town was once an important episcopal seat. Make sure you see its former cathedral, one of the finest churches in the French Alps, boasting beautiful Renaissance stained-glass and one of the oldest organs in France.

🚹 69B5
🛈 Embrun Tourist Office: place Général Dosse (☎ 04 92 43 01 80)

GAP ✪
A lively town and capital of the Hautes Alpes, between Provence and the mountains of the Dauphiné, popular for both summer and winter sports.

🚹 69B5
🛈 Gap Tourist Office: 12 rue Faure du Serre (☎ 04 92 52 56 56)

LA GRAVE ✪✪
One of the oldest and most important mountaineering stations in France, located on the northern edge of the Hautes Alpes, opposite the imposing peak of La Meije (3,983m) – a great alpine challenge for climbers, a depressing number of whom are buried in its churchyard.

🚹 Off map
🛈 La Grave Tourist Office (☎ 04 76 79 90 05)

ST VÉRAN ✪✪
The highest village in Europe at 2,040m, St Véran consists of a handful of wooden chalets dotted over a mountainside near the Italian border. A track leads up through pastures sprinkled with anemones, gentians and other mountain flowers to the tiny chapel of Notre Dame de Clausis, object of a pilgrimage from France and Italy every July.

🚹 Off map
🛈 St Véran Tourist Office (☎ 04 92 45 82 21)

SISTERON ✪
Henri IV described the grandiose citadel of Sisteron (12th–16th century) as 'the most powerful fortress in my kingdom'. High on a rocky bluff, it dominates an unusually contrastive landscape, with the harsh Dauphiné mountains to the north and a rich valley to the south. The strategic importance of the town was re-emphasised as recently as 1944 when it suffered Allied air attacks. The citadel's guardroom contains a museum of local wartime resistance.

🚹 69A4
🛈 Sisteron Tourist Office: Hotel de Ville (☎ 04 92 61 12 03)
La Citadelle
☎ 04 92 61 12 03
🕐 Apr–mid Nov, daily 10–12, 2:30–5:30
♿ Few 💵 Moderate

Alpes-Maritimes

This dramatic stretch of vivid blue coastline with its chic cities, sandy beaches, craggy corniches and fishing villages, has long attracted a rich assortment of actors, artists, writers and royalty to its shores. The luxury high-rise hotels, designer shops and terrace cafés of the smartest Riviera resorts – Cannes, Nice and Monaco – exude a carefree *joie de vivre*, basking in the scorching Mediterranean sun, while their ports overflow with millionaire's yachts. After all, this is the home of the rich and famous...the world's most sophisticated holiday playground.

If it weren't for the steep cliffs that plunge down to the sea between Nice and Menton, it would be easy to forget that 80 per cent of the Alpes-Maritimes are composed of mountains. This is a region of wild, unexplored landscapes, whose slumbering villages – Biot, Saorge, St Paul-de-Vence – offer visitors a chance to sample the true *douceur de vivre* of rural Provence.

'Thirst for the sun!
Thirst for the sand!
Thirst for the clocks that
run slow!'

JACQUES-HENRI LARTIGUE

Nice

Nice is capital of the Alpes-Maritimes département, the Riviera's largest and most interesting city and France's largest tourist resort. Yet despite its status, it remains a friendly place, full of Mediterranean character, with its own dialect (lenga nissarda), its own delicious cuisine (▶ 36–7) and a unique past.

A yachtsman's view of Nice, from the old port

Nice was originally founded by the Greeks in the 4th century BC. Then the Romans had a settlement at Cimiez, later ruined by Saracens. Nice began to thrive again in the Middle Ages, first under the Counts of Provence, then under the Italian Dukes of Savoy. Only unified with France in 1860, it retains a strong Italianate character, combining Italian temperament and lifestyle with French finesse and savoir faire.

Thanks mainly to the English, by the 1860s Nice was already Europe's most fashionable winter retreat, and exuberant *belle epoque* hotels sprang up along the fashionable palm-lined waterfront, aptly named the Promenade des Anglais. Nearby, the alleyways and markets of the *vieille ville* contrast boldly with the broad boulevards and designer shops of the modern city around the handsome main square, place Masséna. The entire city is cradled by the vineclad foothills of the Maritime Alps.

This delightful setting has attracted many artists over the years. As a result, Nice is blessed with more museums and galleries than any French town outside Paris.

A Walk Around Nice Vieille Ville

Start at the western end of cours Saleya.

This square is where Nice's famous outdoor flower, fruit and vegetable market is held (▶ 81), an ideal place to hear the local patois and to taste local delicacies of *socca*, *pissaladière* and other local delicacies.

Head east past the Palace of the former Dukes of Savoy and the Italianate 18th-century Chapelle de la Misericorde to the yellow house at the end of the square, where Matisse once lived. Turn left into rue Gilly then continue along rue Droite, past Palais Lescaris.

Rue Droite contains some of the old town's top galleries and Provence's best bread shops (*Espuno* ▶ 107). Palais Lascaris, an ornate 17th-century Genoese-style mansion, houses the Musée des Arts et Traditions Populaires, containing sumptuous period paintings, furnishings and *trompe l'oeil* ceilings.

Continue straight on until Place St-François and the early morning fish market.

Unusually, this is an *inland* fish market but, before the River Paillon was filled in, fishermen used to land here to sell their catch.

Continue down rue St Francois. Bear right into rue du Collet, left at Place Centrale along rue Centrale, then right into rue Mascoïnat until you reach Place Rossetti.

Place Rossetti is dominated by the beautiful Baroque Cathédrale Ste-Réparate, with its emerald dome of Niçoise tiles. Enjoy a coffee in one of the cafés here or an ice cream from Fenocchio's (▶ 99).

Leave the square along rue Ste Reparate. At the end, turn right into rue de la Prefecture.

The great violinist Niccolò Paganini lived and died at No 23.

A right turn opposite Paganini's house into rue St Gaëtan takes you back to the cours Saleya.

Distance
2km

Time
1–2 hours, depending on shopping, museum and church visits

Start/end point
cours Saleya
✚ 85B2
🚌 All buses

Lunch
La Criée (££)
✉ 22 cours Saleya
☎ 04 93 85 49 99

The colours of old Nice – sunny terracotta reds and cool green shutters

79

It comes as a surprise to find a Russian church at the heart of Nice

What to See in Nice

CATHÉDRALE ORTHODOXE RUSSE ✪

This magnificent pink and grey Russian Orthodox church, crowned by six gleaming green onion-shaped cuppolas, was built by Tzar Nicolas II in 1903 in memory of his son Nicolas, who is buried in the grounds. Brimming with precious icons, frescoes and treasures, the church still conducts regular services in Russian.

CIMIEZ ✪✪

Nice's smartest residential area owes much of its original cachet to Queen Victoria who used to winter here at the once-palatial Hotel Regina. Near by lies the newly-excavated Roman settlement and a small **archaeological museum** and a 16th-century Franciscan Monastery and Church, containing three masterpieces by Nice-born primitive painter Louis Bréa. Dufy and Matisse lie buried in the adjacent cemetery. Every July, Europe's leading international Jazz Festival is held in Cimiez, in the beautiful olive grove beside the Musée Matisse.

MUSÉE D'ART MODERNE ET D'ART CONTEMPORAIN (MAMAC) ✪✪✪

The museum's collections trace the history of French and American avant-garde from the 'sixties to the present: New Realists, American Pop Art, Fluxus, Minimalism and the Nice School, in particular its founder Yves Klein. The building, itself a 'museum-monument', is a masterpiece of modern art with memorable views from its rooftop terraces. On Fridays at 9:30PM, the illumination of Klein's *Mur de Feu* (Wall of Fire) on the roof is a sight to behold.

✚ 85B2
✉ avenue Nicolas II
🕐 10–12, 3–6. Closed Sun AM
🚌 5,7,17,23,24
♿ Good 🎫 Moderate

✚ 85B2
Musée Archéologique de Cimiez
✉ 160 avenue des Arènes
☎ 04 93 81 59 57
🕐 Apr–Sep, 10–12, 2–6; Oct–Mar, 10–1, 2–5. Closed Mon and hols
🚌 15,17, 20, 22, 25
♿ Few 🎫 Expensive
❓ Guided tours 1st Wed of month at 3PM

✚ 85B2
✉ promenade des Arts
☎ 04 93 62 61 62
🕐 11–6 (till 10 Fri). Closed Tue and hols
🚌 1, 2, 3, 4, 5, 6, 7, 9, 10, 14, 16, 17, 25
🍴 Cafés & restaurants (££)
♿ Excellent 🎫 Expensive

MUSÉE NATIONAL MESSAGE BIBLIQUE MARC CHAGALL 😊😊😊

Located in the heart of a Mediterranean garden, this striking modern museum was specially built to house Chagall's 'Biblical Message' – a series of 17 monumental canvases evoking the Garden of Eden, Moses and other Old Testament themes – and was opened by the artist himself in 1973. He also created the mosaic and the beautiful blue stained-glass windows in the concert hall. Other works, including paintings, etchings, lithographs, sculptures and tapestries, were donated to the museum after Chagall's death in 1985, making this the most important permanent collection of his work.

Musée national
Message Biblique
Marc Chagall

🔹 85B2
✉ avenue Docteur Ménard
☎ 04 93 53 87 20
🕐 Jul–Sep, 10–6;
Oct–Jun, 10–5.
Closed Tue, 1 Jan, 1
May, 25 Dec
🍴 Garden café
Apr–Oct (£)
🚌 15
♿ Excellent
💷 Very expensive
↔ Cimiez (➤ 80)
❓ Shop, library,
concert hall.
Reserve guided
tours in advance

The remarkable Chagall Museum is a must for all

MUSÉE MATISSE (➤ 22, TOP TEN)

PROMENADE DES ANGLAIS 😊😊

As its name suggests, this palm-lined promenade which graciously sweeps round the Baie des Anges (Bay of Angels) was constructed at the expense of Nice's wealthy English residents in 1822, so they could stroll along the shoreline. Today, it is bordered by a highway of *autoroute* proportions and the white wedding-cake style architecture of the luxury *belle époque* hotels such as the world-famous Negresco (➤ 103) are now juxtaposed with ugly concrete apartment blocks. Don't miss the **Palais Masséna**, next to the Negresco, now a museum devoted to regional history and including Napoleonic mementos, or the remarkable collections of the nearby **International Museum of Naïve Art**.

🔹 85B2
Palais Masséna
✉ 35 Promenade des Anglais
☎ 04 93 62 61 62
🕐 10–12, 2–6 (till 10 Fri).
Closed Mon and some hols
🚌 3, 6, 7, 9, 10, 12, 14, 22
♿ Few 💷 Expensive
International Museé D'art Naïf
✉ Château Ste-Hélène
☎ 04 93 71 78 33
🕐 10–12, 2–6. Closed Tue
and some hols
🚌 6, 9, 10, 12, 23, 24, 26, 34
♿ Few 💷 Moderate

VIEILLE VILLE AND COURS SALEYA 😊😊😊

Old Nice – a maze of dark narrow streets, festooned with flowers and laundry and brimming with cafés, hidden squares and bustling markets. Dismissed as a dangerous slum in the 1970s, this is now the trendiest part of Nice, lively day and night, especially the cours Saleya. This spacious, sunny square is scene of one of France's top fruit and vegetable markets – the tastes, fragrances and colours of Provence and Italy are a veritable feast for the senses. By night, cafés and restaurants fill the *cours*, making it one of Nice's most animated night spots.

🔹 85B2
🚌 All buses
❓ Fruit and vegetable
market: Tue–Sun AM;
flower market (all day
except Sun PM); flea
market: Mon

Monaco

After the Vatican, Monaco is the world's smallest sovereign state, a 195-hectare spotlessly clean strip of sky-scraper-covered land squeezed between sea and mountains. There are no taxes, and the world's highest incomes attract the rich and famous.

Monaco is the name of the Principality, and also of the district on the peninsula to the south, containing the old town with its narrow streets and pastel-coloured houses, a startling contrast to the newer high-rise district of Monte Carlo, centred round its glitzy casino and designer shops. With so much evident wealth and glamour, it is hard to imagine Monaco's turbulent past, at various times occupied by the French, the Spanish and the Dukes of Savoy. The present ruling king is Prince Rainier III, whose family, the Grimaldis, have ruled Monaco for 700 years-the world's oldest reigning monarchy.

The Grimaldis once held sway over an area, which extended along the coast and included Menton and Roquebrune. However, their high taxes provoked a revolt, and the principality shrank to its present size. Facing a financial crisis, Charles III of Monaco decided to turn to gambling for his revenue, not by betting the royal reserves, but by opening a casino. Such was its success, that taxes were soon abolished altogether.

The ornate casino

What to See in Monaco

CASINO ✪✪✪

Even if you are not a gambler, it is worth visiting the world's most famous casino, designed in 1878 by Charles Garnier, architect of the Paris Opéra, to see the opulent *belle époque* interior and tiny, highly ornate opera house, the Salle Garnier, which has been graced by many of the world's most distinguished opera singers. The dazzlingly-illuminated Place du Casino by night is a must-see. The Café de Paris and Hôtel de Paris are worth a look too.

THE CÔTE D'AZUR

Loup ▲1777m

St Martin-du-Var

Utelle

Col de Brous
879m

Saorge

Col de Braus
1002m

Levens

Breil-sur-Roya

Gorges du Loup

Vence

L'Escarène

Sospel

N85

Var

A8/E80

Grasse

St-Paul-de-Vence

Biot

Cagnes-sur-Mer

Monte-Carlo

Menton

Mandelieu-la-Napoule

Mougins

Villefranche

NICE

MC

Roquebrune-Cap-Martin

A8/E80

Antibes

Cap Ferrat

Cannes

Juan-les-Pins

Le Trayas

Îles de Lérins

Cap d'Antibes

Côte d'Azur

0   10   20   30 km

N

A   B   C

CATHÉDRALE ✪

Built in 1875 (and funded by casino profits!), this ostentatious neo-Romanesque cathedral stands on the site of a 13th-century church dedicated to St Nicolas. Among its treasures are two 16th-century retables by Niçoise artist Louis Bréa and tombs of the former Princes of Monaco and the much-mourned Princess Grace.

✚ 83B2
✉ 4 rue Colonel Bellando de Castro
☎ 04 93 30 88 13
♿ Good
🎟 Free

MUSÉE OCÉANOGRAPHIQUE ✪✪✪

Founded by Prince Albert I in 1910 to house his remarkable collections of marine flora, fauna, nautical instruments and a 20-m whale skeleton, and located in a grandiose building on a sheer cliff high above the Mediterranean, this spectacular aquarium and museum of marine science is the finest of its kind in the world. Marine explorer Jacques Cousteau set up his research centre here and his remarkable films are regularly screened in the museum's cinema.

✚ 83B2
✉ avenue Saint-Martin
☎ 04 93 15 36 00
🕐 Oct–Mar, 9:30–7; Apr–Jun & Sep, 9–7; Jul–Aug, 9–8; Nov–Feb, 10–6. Closed 19 May
🍽 Restaurant & bar
♿ Good
🎟 Very expensive

PALAIS DU PRINCE ✪

In summer, when Prince Rainier is away, guided tours take visitors through the priceless treasures of the State Appartments and the small Musée Napoléon in the south wing of the palace. When he is in residence, the royal colours are flown from the tower and visitors must content themselves with the Changing of the Guard ceremony (daily at 11:55AM).

✚ 83B2
✉ place du Palais
☎ 04 93 25 18 31
🕐 June–Sept, 9:30–6:30; Oct 10–5. Closed Nov–May
♿ Few
🎟 Very expensive
🔄 Cathédrale

What to See in Alpes–Maritimes

ANTIBES

Antibes was founded in the 5th century BC as a Greek trading post, and centuries later was controlled by the Dukes of Savoy until the 18th-century. Napoleon was held prisoner here in 1794 in Vauban's mighty 17th century Fort Carée on the eastern edge of town. Today, its massive ramparts protect Old Antibes from flooding. The Grimaldi family ruled from the 12th-to 16th-century seafront château, which today houses one of the world's finest Picasso collections (► 23).

Old Antibes, which lies hidden behind the ramparts, is a veritable maze of cobbled, winding lanes overflowing with shops, restaurants and bars. Don't miss the bustling morning market in the cours Masséna or the craft market on Friday and Sunday afternoons (also Tuesdays and Thursdays in summer). On the waterfront, the Port Vauban Yacht Harbour boasts some of the Côte d'Azur's most luxurious yachts.

BIOT

Five kilometres north of Antibes lies the charming hilltop village of Biot – a mass of steep cobbled lanes lined with quaint sand-coloured houses capped by orange-tiled roofs, leading up to the famous arcaded main square. The streets are decorated with huge earthenware jars ablaze with geraniums and tropical plants as, for centuries, Biot has been a thriving pottery centre. It is also known for its gold and silverwork, ceramics, olivewood-carving and thriving glassworks. Visitors can watch glass-blowers at the Verrerie de Biot demonstrating their unique *verre bullé* (bubble glass).

Near by, the striking **Musée Fernand Léger**, with its huge brilliantly-coloured mosaic façade and monumental stained-glass windows, was founded in 1959 in memory of Cubist painter Fernand Léger who lived at Biot for a short time and inspired the growth of the craft workshops here. The museum contains nearly 400 of his works, including ceramics, tapestries, stained glass and mosaics.

CAGNES-SUR-MER

Cagnes is divided into three: the old fishing quarter and main beach area of Cros-de-Cagnes; Cagnes-Ville, the commercial centre with its smart racecourse beside the sea; and Haut-de-Cagnes. This inviting hilltop village, with its brightly-coloured houses smothered in bougainvillaea, mimosa and geraniums, is crowned by a 14th-century château, built by Admiral Rainer Grimaldi as a pirate lookout. The castle contains several permanent exhibitions including the Olive Tree Museum and the Museum of Modern Mediterranean Art, exhibiting works by Chagall, Matisse and Renoir, Cagnes's most famous artist.

83A2

Antibes Tourist Office: 11 place du Général de Gaulle (☎ 04 92 90 53 00)

↔ Biot (► below), Cagnes (► 84), Cannes (► 85), Grasse (► 88), Mougins (► 89), Nice (► 78), St-Paul-de-Vence (► 89), Vence (► 90)

83A2

Biot Tourist Office: place de la Chapelle (☎ 04 93 65 05 85)

↔ Antibes (► 84), Cagnes (► 84); Cannes (► 85); Grasse (► 88); Mougins (► 89); Nice (► 78); St-Paul-de-Vence (► 89); Vence (► 90)

Musée Léger

✉ 09410 Biot

☎ 04 92 91 50 30

🕐 Summer 10–12:30, 2–8; winter 10–12:30, 2–5:30. Closed Tue

♿ Good 💷 Expensive

❓ Phone in advance to arrange guided tours

83A2

Cagnes Tourist Office: 6 boulevard Maréchal Juin (☎ 04 93 20 61 64)

Musée Renoir

✉ 19 chemin des collettes

☎ 04 93 20 61 07

🕐 May–Oct, 10–12, 2–6; Dec–Apr, 10–12, 2–5. Closed Tue & Nov

♿ Few 💷 Moderate

CANNES ⊗

Think Cannes, think movies and film stars, expensive boutiques, palatial hotels and paparazzi! After all, it is one of the world's most chic resorts, twinned with Beverly Hills and, within France, second only to Paris for shopping, tourism and major international cultural and business events, including the world-famous Film Festival (▶ 116).

With so much glitz and glamour, it is easy to forget that Cannes was a mere fishing village until 1834 when retired British chancellor Lord Brougham, en route to Nice, was enchanted by its warm climate and quaint setting, and built a villa here to spend the winter months. Soon hundreds of other aristocrats and royals followed his example. Before long hotels began to spring up along the waterfront. However, it was not until the 1930s that Cannes became a summer resort, made fashionable by visiting Americans. By the 1950s mass summer tourism had taken off and has been the life-blood of Cannes ever since.

The town is divided into two parts. The Vieux Port and old Roman town of *Canois Castrum* (now known as Le Suquet) situated on a small hill to the west, is crowned by an 11th-century castle and watchtower affording a sweeping coastal vista. To the east, modern Cannes is built round La Croisette, Europe's most elegant sea promenade, lined with palms and flanked by designer shops, grand belle-époque hotels and the sparkling Bay of Cannes with its golden beaches (of imported sand to cover the natural pebble), each with their tidy rows of coloured parasols and mattresses.

➕ 83A2
ℹ️ Cannes Tourist Office: Palais des Festivals, Esplanade du Président-Georges-Pompidou (☎ 04 93 01 01)
↔️ Antibes (▶ 84); Biot (▶ 84); Mougins (▶ 89)
❓ International Film Festival in May (▶ 116). Cinemas screen films from early morning well into the night, but it is difficult to get tickets unless you are accompanied by Bardot or Bond 007

The Old Port – a reminder of Canne's origins as a humble fishing village

85

🔲 83B2

ℹ️ Cap Ferrat Tourist Office:
06230 St Jean-Cap-Ferrat
(☎ 04 93 76 08 90)

🔲 The Corniches (▶ 86),
Èze (▶ 87), Nice (▶ 78),
Villefranche- sur-Mer
(▶ 90)

Villa Ephrussi de Rothschild

✉️ Chemin du Musée Saint-
Jean-Cap-Ferrat

☎ 04 93 01 33 09

🕐 15 Feb–1 Nov 10–6 (till 7
Jul/Aug); 2 Nov–14 Feb
2–6 (weekdays), 10–6
(weekends & school
hols); Closed 25 Dec

🍴 Salon de thé (££)

♿ Few

💰 Very expensive

❓ Guided tours available

🔲 83B2

🔲 Nice (▶ 78), Monaco
(▶ 82), Èze (▶ 87)

*Cary Grant and Grace
Kelly on the Corniches*

CAP FERRAT ⭐

The most desirable address on the Côte d'Azur – the 'Peninsula of Billionaires' – with its huge villas hidden in sub-tropical gardens, has long been a favourite haunt of the rich and famous including King Leopold II of Belgium, Somerset Maugham, Edith Piaf, the Duke and Duchess of Windsor, Charlie Chaplin and David Niven. A delightful coast path from Villefranche around the cape past countless tiny azure inlets (ideal for a refreshing dip), makes a pleasant stroll before lunch in the former fishing village of St-Jean-Cap-Ferrat.

Cap Ferrat's finest villa – considered by many the finest on the Riviera – is the **Villa Île de France**, a rose-pink *belle époque* palace constructed by the flamboyant Baroness Béatrice Ephrussi de Rothschild (1864–1934), set in immaculate formal gardens with wonderful sea views. The remarkable interior is lavishly decorated with rare furniture (including some pieces that once belonged to Marie Antoinette), set off by rich carpets, tapestries and an eclectic collection of rare *objets d'art*.

THE CORNICHES ⭐⭐⭐

Three famous *corniches* (cliff-roads) traverse the most scenic and most mountainous stretch of the Côte d'Azur from Nice to Menton via Monaco. Called *La Grande* (D2564), *La Moyenne* (N7) and *L'Inférieure*, they each zig-zag their way along vertiginous ledges at three different elevations. *La Grande Corniche*, at the highest level, was first constructed by Napoleon and is by far the best choice for picnickers and lovers of plants and wildlife.

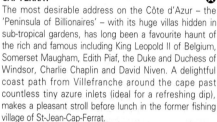

The lowest route (*Corniche Inférieure*) follows the coastal contours through all the seaside resorts, and is best avoided in the main tourist season of July and August.

The steep *Corniche Moyenne* in the middle is undoubtedly the most dramatic - a cliff-hanging route with hair-raising bends, sudden tunnels and astounding views, frequently used for car commercials and movie car-chases.

ÈZE ✪✪✪

Èze, the most strikingly-situated and best-preserved ancient Provençal *village perché*, stands high on a rocky pinnacle ten minutes drive from Nice and Monaco. Frequently called the *Nid d'Aigle* (Eagle's Nest), it boasts spectacular views over the entire Riviera as far as Corsica.

Tall, golden stone houses and a labyrinth of tiny vaulted passages and stairways climb steeply up to the ruins of the once massive Saracen fortress 429m above sea level, surrounded by an **exotic garden**, bristling with magnificent cacti, succulents and rare palms. Take time to explore the countless craft shops housed in small caves within the rock – tiny treasure troves of antiques, ceramics, pewter-work and olivewood carvings. At the foot of the hill, The two perfume factories of Galimard and Fragonard both contain fascinating museums.

🔟 Off map
🛈 Èze Tourist Office: place de Gaulle (☎ 04 93 41 26 00)
🔁 Cap Ferrat (▶ 86), The Corniches (▶ 86), Menton (▶ 88), Monaco (▶ 82), Nice (▶ 78), Villefranche-sur-Mer (▶ 90)

Jardin Exotique
✉ rue du Château
☎ 04 93 41 10 30
🕐 9–12, 2–dusk
♿ None
✋ Moderate

➕ 83A3

ℹ️ Grasse Tourist Office: 3 Place de la Foux (☎ 04 93 36 03 56)

↔️ Cannes (► 85), Mougins (► 89)

Maison Fragonard

✉️ 20 boulevard Fragonard, 06130 Grasse

☎ 04 93 36 44 65

🕐 Daily

♿ Good

🎫 Free

Studio des Fragrances Galimard

✉️ route de Pégomas, 06332 Grasse

☎ 04 93 09 20 00

🕐 Daily by appointment

♿ Good

🎫 Free, but very expensive to create your own perfume

GRASSE ✪✪

For 400 years Grasse has been the capital of the perfume industry. Until recently 85 per cent of the world's flower essence was created here, and this sleepy, fragrance-filled town is still France's leading centre for the cut flower market. Learn about the history and alchemy of the perfume industry at the Musée International de la Parfumerie, or take a guided tour around **Maison Fragonard**, Grasse's largest perfume factory, named after a local artist Jean-Honoré Fragonard (1732–1806). Or why not create your own personal fragrance at Galimard's **Studio des Fragrances**?

Did you know?

Grasse was originally a tannery town, where, in the 16th century, Italian glove-makers began to use local flowers to perfume leather gloves, a fashion made popular by Catherine of Médici. Acre upon acre of lavender, mimosa, roses, jasmine and jonquils were cultivated and Grasse soon became the centre of the French perfume industry, creating the essences for Chanel, Givenchy and many other famous brands.

Grasse perfume bottles

➕ 83C2

ℹ️ Menton Tourist Office: Palais de l'Europe, avenue Boyer (☎ 04 93 57 57 00)

↔️ Èze (► 87), Monaco (► 82), Saorge (► 89)

MENTON ✪✪

Just 1.6km from the border, France's most Italianate resort, with its steep jumble of tall, honey-coloured houses, is wedged between a sweeping palm-lined bay and a dramatic mountain backdrop. Menton is France's warmest town, boasting an annual 300 days of sun and resulting in a town bursting with semi-tropical gardens. Menton is also the 'lemon capital of the world', smothered in citrus groves. Every February a spectacular Lemon Festival takes place in the Jardins Biovès (► 60–1).

Make sure you see the medieval old town, with its two magnificent ice cream-coloured churches – St Michel's

Church and the Chapel of the White Penitents – and the beautiful old cemetery beyond with its striking sea views. Other notable sights include the Jean Cocteau Museum, the Musée de la Préhistoire Régional, boasting the remains of 'Menton Man' (30,000 BC), and Palais Carnolès, the sumptuous 18th-century summer residence of the princes of Monaco, now Menton's main art museum.

Menton's proximity to Italy is apparent in its architecture (and abundance of pasta restaurants)

MOUGINS ✪✪

At first glance Mougins appears a typical Provençal hill village, but inside its medieval ramparts lies one of the Riviera's smartest villages. Past residents include Jacques Brel, Yves Saint Laurent, Catherine Deneuve and Picasso, photos of whom are displayed in the **Musée de la Photographie**.

The real attraction today, however, is the sheer volume of high-class restaurants. Try Le Relais, La Ferme de Mougins or, for a real treat, Le Moulin de Mougins (► 98) just outside the village is considered one of the most prestigious in the world.

➕ 83A2
ℹ Mougins Tourist Office: avenue Charles Mallet (☎ 04 93 75 87 67)

Musée de la Photographie
✉ Porte Sarrazine, Mougins
☎ 04 93 75 85 67
🕐 Daily 1–7; Jul–Aug 2–11. Closed Tue
♿ Few
▣ Moderate

SAORGE ✪

As you climb the panoramic Roya Valley into the mountains from the coast, the medieval listed village of Saorge is a magnificent sight. Hanging 200m above the river, its tidy rows of Italian slate-roofed ochre and blue houses rise in tiers, in the typical style of a *village empilé* (stacked village). Once a Piedmontese border stronghold, Saorge was taken by the French in 1794, but has still retained its unique customs and dialect. Outside the village, the elegant baroque **Franciscan monastery** offers precipitous views into the valley.

➕ 83C3
ℹ Saorge Tourist Office: La Mairie (☎ 04 93 04 51 23)
 Menton (► 88); Monaco (► 82)

Saorge Franciscan Monastery
🕐 Sat 2–4, Sun 10–12, 2–4:30

ST PAUL-DE-VENCE ✪✪✪

Gently draped over a hill close to Cagnes, this picture-postcard *village perché* was appointed a 'Royal Town' in the 16th century by King François – better described today as a tourist honeypot, with coachloads flocking to the Foundation Maeght (► 18) and the smart shops and galleries. However, despite the crowds, it remains one of Provence's most beautiful villages, especially at night when the narrow alleys are lit with tiny lanterns.

➕ 83B3
ℹ St Paul-de-Vence Tourist Office: Maison de la Tour, 2 rue Grande (☎ 04 93 32 86 95)
Antibes (► 84), Biot (► 84), Cagnes (► 84), Nice (► 78), Vence (► 90)

🔲 83A3

ℹ️ Vence Tourist Office: place du Grand-Jardin (☎ 04 93 58 06 38)

↔️ Antibes (➤ 84), Biot (➤ 84), Cagnes (➤ 84), Nice (➤ 78), St-Paul-de-Vence(➤ 89)

Chapelle du Rosaire

✉️ avenue Henri Matisse

☎ 04 93 58 03 26

🕐 Dec–Oct, Tue & Thu 10–12, 3–5

♿ Good

💷 Expensive

The serenity of the Chappelle du rosaire is reflected in Matisse's minimalist lines

🔲 83B2

ℹ️ Villefranche-Sur-Mer Tourist Office: Jardin François Binon (☎ 04 93 01 73 68)

↔️ Cap Ferrat (➤ 86), the Corniches (➤ 86), Èze (➤ 87)

Chapelle St-Pierre

✉️ Port de Villefranche

☎ 04 93 76 90 70

🕐 Tue–Sun 10–12, 2:30–4:30

♿ Good 💷 Moderate

VENCE ✪✪

This delightful old town, only 10km inland from the coast, was once the Roman forum of *Vintium*. In the Middle Ages, it became a bishopric, and its 10th-century cathedral (the smallest in France) is rich in treasures, including Roman tombstones embedded in the walls and a remarkable Chagall mosaic.

Vence has long attracted many artists and, in 1941, Henri Matisse moved here to escape Allied bombing on the coast, but he then fell seriously ill. Dominican sisters nursed him back to health and, as a gift, he built and decorated the tiny **Chapelle du Rosaire** for them. The interior is compelling in its simplicity, with powerful black line-drawings of the Stations of the Cross on white faïence, coloured only by pools of yellow, blue and green light from the enormous stained-glass windows. Matisse worked on this masterpiece well into his 80s, considering it his 'ultimate goal, the culmination of an intense, sincere and difficult endeavour'.

VILLEFRANCHE-SUR-MER ✪✪

Considering its proximity to Nice and Monte Carlo, Villefranche remains surprisingly unspoilt, little changed over the centuries since it was founded in the 14th century as a customs-free port (hence its name). Its picturesque natural harbour is fringed with old red and orange Italianate houses, tempting waterfront bars, cafés and restaurants.

Take time to explore the maze of steep stairways and cavernous vaulted passageways which climb from the harbour through the *Vieille Ville*, and the sturdy 16th-century citadel, with galleries of paintings and sculptures by local artists, including Picasso and Mirò. By the quay, the tiny 14th-century **Chapelle de St Pierre**, once used to store fishing nets, was decorated in 1957 with frescoes by Ville franche's most famous resident, Jean Cocteau.

Where To...

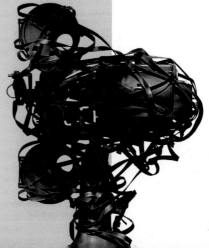

Vaucluse

Opening Times and Prices
Prices are approximate, based on a three-course meal for one without drinks and service:

£ = under F150
££ = F150–F300
£££ = over F300

The restaurants on the following pages are all open for lunch and dinner daily unless otherwise stated.

A Taste of the Past
Marylin and Mary-Christine spent six months researching the old Provençal recipes of their grandmothers, in order to create the true 'cuisine de Provence du temps jadis'. They now painstakingly recreate these unusual dishes in their tiny restaurant in a backstreet of Avignon, producing a weekly changing menu including such delicacies as cold zucchini soup with basil, rabbit *bouillabaisse*, honey, lavender and spiced-bread ice-cream.

Avignon
Le Belgocargo (£)
Belgian restaurant offering 16 different types of *moule frites* on a huge sunny terrace.
✉ 10 place des Châtaignes ☎ 04 90 85 72 99 🕐 Closed Sun in winter

Christian Etienne (£££)
One of Avignon's top gourmet temples in a 14th-century palace beside the Palais des Papes. Try the fish, foie gras and truffle specialities.
✉ 10 rue de Mons ☎ 04 90 86 16 50 🕐 Closed Sat lunch & Sun

Le Cloître (£)
Savoury or sweet pancakes washed down with a bowl of cider, in a cosy traditional restaurant.
✉ 9 place du Cloître St Pierre ☎ 04 90 85 34 63 🕐 7 days a week 12–2:30, 7–midnight

La Fourchette (££)
A smaller, more relaxed, cheaper offspring of Hiély-Lucullus (▶ below), nonetheless with delicious dishes. Very popular. Reservations essential.
✉ 17 rue Racine ☎ 04 90 85 20 93 🕐 Closed Sat & Sun

Hiély-Lucullus (£££)
Avignon's top gastronomic palace, rated as one of France's top 50 restaurants.
✉ 5 rue de la République ☎ 04 90 86 17 07 🕐 Closed Mon, Tue lunchtime in high season, & Jan

Le Jujubier (£)
An authentic taste of ancient Provence (▶ panel).
✉ 14 rue du Roi René ☎ 04 90 86 64 08 🕐 Lunchtimes only Mon–Fri. Closed Sat & Sun

Simple Simon (£)
This quaint *olde worlde* English tearoom serves steak and kidney pie, Bakewell tart and even Christmas pudding.
✉ 26 rue petite Fusterie ☎ 04 90 86 62 70 🕐 11:45–7

La Table de Patrick (£)
Typical bistro atmosphere with chalkboard menus, red-check cloths and candles. Tasty French cuisine, including a vast all-you-can-eat lunchtime *crudité* menu for F50. Excellent value.
✉ 20–22 rue du Chapeau Rouge ☎ 04 90 86 10 46 🕐 Closed Sun lunch in winter

Tapalocas (£)
An authentic spanish-style bodega, with tapas dishes at F12 each.
✉ 10 rue galante ☎ 04 90 82 56 84

Bonnieux
Le Fournil (££)
A rustic restaurant at the heart of the Lubéron, with a charming fountain-splashed terrace for *al fresco* dining.
✉ 5 place Carnot ☎ 04 90 75 83 62 🕐 Closed Mon & Tue lunch

Cavaillon
Prévot (£££)
Chef Jean-Jaques Prévot's lavish dining room of chandeliers, tapestries and mirrors is matched by equally rich cuisine. Try his *artichaut soufflé* and his succulent Cavaillon melon desserts.
✉ 353 avenue Verdun ☎ 04 90 71 32 42 🕐 Closed Sun evening & Mon

Châteauneuf-du-Pape
La Mère Germaine (££)
One of the the village's most

popular restaurants. The dazzling wine list includes all the best *crus* of the appellation.

✉ avenue du Commandant-Lemaître ☎ 04 90 83 54 37 🕐 Closed Sun evening, Mon & Jan

Violès

Domaine de la Tuilerie (£)

Hearty home cooking in an old farmhouse. Reservation essential.

✉ Violès, west of Gigondas ☎ 04 90 70 92 89 🕐 Closed Tue

Gordes

Le Mas Fourteron (£££)

A true taste of Provence in an 18th-century farmhouse, courtesy of Elisabeth Bourgeois' imaginative and refined regional cuisine.

✉ Chemin Saint-Blaise ☎ 04 90 72 00 16 🕐 Closed Sun evening & Mon

Lacoste

Café de France (£)

Cheap and cheerful with *salade Niçoise* or omelette and fries for under F100.

✉ Le Village ☎ 04 90 75 82 25 🕐 Lunchtime only

Le Simiane (££)

Cosy restaurant at the heart of the Lubéron, made famous by Peter Mayle in *A Year in Provence* (▶ panel).

✉ rue Sous-Barri ☎ 04 90 75 83 31 🕐 Closed Wed

Lourmarin

Le Moulin de Lourmarin (£££)

Four extravagant menus in a beautiful converted oil-mill. A veritable feast for the senses.

✉ rue du Temple ☎ 04 90 68 06 69 🕐 Closed Tue & Wed lunchtime & mid-Jan–mid-Feb

Orange

Le Yaka (£)

Provençal bistro with wooden beams, floral tablecloths, generous portions and a jolly atmosphere near the Antique Theatre.

✉ 24 place Sylvian ☎ 04 90 34 70 03 🕐 Closed Tue evening, Wed & Nov

La Roselière (£)

Rustic restaurant near the Cathedral. The saucissons hanging from the beam overhead become appetizers in this rustic restaurant with a small shady terrace.

✉ 4 rue du Renoyer ☎ 04 90 34 50 42 🕐 Closed all day Wed, Thu lunchtime

Roussillon

David (£££)

Admire the red cliffs of ochre from the terrace of this delightful restaurant. Wholesome Provençal cuisine.

✉ place de la Poste ☎ 04 90 05 60 13 🕐 Closed Mon

Seguret

Le Mesclun (££)

Intimate restaurant serving regional dishes, washed down with Côtes-du-Rhône wines, accompanied by sweeping views of the Comtat Venaissin.

✉ rue des Poternes ☎ 04 90 46 93 43 🕐 Closed Mon, & Oct–Easter

Venasque

Auberge la Fontaine (£–££)

The restaurant here has a cosy log fire in winter and classical concerts once a month. Try the *gigot d'agneau de Venasque* and other local dishes.

✉ place de la Fontaine ☎ 04 90 66 02 96 🕐 Closed Mon & Wed

A 'Meal' In Provence

'By 12:30 the little stone-walled restaurant [Le Simiane] was full. There were some serious stomachs to be seen… The proprietor of the restaurant… quivered with enthusiasm as he rhapsodised over the menu: foie gras, lobster mousse, beef *en croûte*, salads dressed in virgin oil, hand-picked cheeses, desserts of a miraculous lightness, *digestifs*. It was a gastronomic aria which he performed at each table.'

(*A Year in Provence* by Peter Mayle)

Bouches-du-Rhône

A Prickly Plateful

Don't be surprised if you are presented with a plate of shiny, black, seaweed-draped *oursin* (sea urchins) as they are considered a great delicacy in Cassis. Simply scrape out the rosy-pink insides and eat raw with a glass of the prestigious *vin de Cassis*. Legend has it that God felt sorry for the people of Cassis and shed a tear which landed on a vine, giving birth to a dry white wine of a pale green tint, with a bouquet of heather and rosemary.

Aix-En-Provence

Autour D'une Tarte (£)

Generous slices of sweet and savoury tarts make a perfect snack. Takeaway also available.

✉ 13 rue Gaston de Saporta ☎ 04 42 96 52 12 🕐 Lunch only. Closed Sun

Aux P'tits Soufflés (£)

Over 50 different types of soufflé. Be daring and try the snail one!

✉ 9 rue Félibre Gaut ☎ 04 42 26 02 79 🕐 Closed Sun, Mon

Chez Gu & Fils (£££)

Recommended by Gault et Millau and Peter Mayle, with market-fresh culinary creations, checked tablecloths and a cosy log fire in winter.

✉ 3 rue Frederic Mistral ☎ 04 42 26 75 12 🕐 Closed Sun

Jacquou le Croquant (£)

Tasty *tourtons* (wholewheat pancakes) with different fillings in an intimate non-smoking bistro.

✉ 2 rue de l'Aumône Vieille ☎ 04 42 27 37 19 🕐 Closed Sun & Mon in winter; Mon & Sun lunch in summer

La Masion des Fondues (££)

No need to go to the mountains for a fondue. You will find 50 different ones here, from the traditional *bourguignone* to irresistible chocolate and chestnut cream dips.

✉ 13 rue de la Verrerie ☎ 04 42 63 07 78 🕐 Evening only.

L'Oeuf Gourmand (£)

Cheap, cheerful omelette specialities from F27.

✉ 5 rue Entrecastreaux ☎ 04 42 27 06 94 🕐 Closed Sun & Mon lunch

Unic Bar (£)

A perfect bar for people watching, opposite Aix's colourful fruit and vegetable market. In summer, fresh fruit juice is the speciality.

✉ 40 rue Vauvenargues ☎ 04 42 96 38 28

Yamato (££)

A small, authentic and reasonably priced Japanese restaurant.

✉ 4 rue Lieutaut ☎ 04 42 38 52 65 🕐 Evening only

Arles

L'Affenage (££)

Traditional fare in the converted stables of a charming 18th-century coaching inn.

✉ 4 rue Molière ☎ 04 90 96 07 67 🕐 Closed Wed eve, Sun

L'Escaladou (£)

Authentic, down-to-earth Arlésien restaurant packed with locals. Hearty helpings of *aïoli*, Arles sausages and *boeuf gardian* (▶ 36/7).

✉ 23 rue Porte de Laure ✉ 04 90 96 70 43 🕐 Closed Sun

Le Médiéval (££)

Barbecued specialities in a converted 12th century abbey.

✉ 9 rue Truchet ☎ 04 90 96 65 77 🕐 Evening only. Closed Tue.

Aubagne

Le Parc (£)

Bright, sunny Provençal-style restaurant opening onto a cool, shady park.

✉ Avenue du 21 août 1944, Parc Jean moulin ☎ 04 42 84 15 14 🕐 Closed Sun.

Le Vaccarès (££)

One of Arles top restaurants; Enjoy some of the region's finest fare, accompanied by the best Rhône wines, on a shady balcony overlooking the place du Forum.

✉ 9 rue Favorin ☎ 04 90 96 06 17 🕐 Closed Sun evening, Mon

Vitamine (£)

A vegetarian paradise. Stacks of salad and pasta in a light, airy café.

✉ 16 rue du Docteur-Fanton ☎ 04 90 93 77 36 🕐 Closed Sat evening & Sun

Les Baux

L'Oustau de Baumanière (£££)

One of France's finest hotel restaurants, visited by royalty, politicians and celebrities.

✉ Val d'Enfer ☎ 04 90 54 33 07 🕐 Closed Wed & mid-Jan–Feb

Cassis

La Voute (£)

A heaped pan of *moules frites* washed down with *vin de Cassis* on the waterfront. Excellent value.

✉ 2 quai des Baux ☎ 04 42 01 73 33 🕐 Closed Sun evening & Mon

Fontvieille

Le Patio (££)

Traditional yet imaginative cuisine in an old farm with a pretty flower-splashed patio.

✉ 117 route du Nord ☎ 04 90 54 73 10 🕐 Closed Wed in winter; Wed lunchtime in summer

Marseille

Le Mas (£)

Early birds meet night owls here for a coffee and a snack at dawn.

✉ 4 rue Lilli ☎ 04 91 33 25 90 🕐 Open 24 hours. Closed Aug 🚌 bus 31, 33, 34, 41, 80, 81

Le Miramar (£££)

The ultimate *Bouillabaisse* beside the old port (▶ panel).

✉ 12 quai du Port, 13002 Marseille ☎ 04 91 91 10 40 🕐 Closed Sun 🚇 Metro 1 (Vieux Port)

Le Roi du Couscous (£)

The best couscous in town.

✉ 63 rue de la République ☎ 04 91 91 45 46 🕐 Closed Mon 🚌 bus 35, 57, 61

Toinou (£–££)

Home of Francis Rouquier, France's champion shellfish opener.

✉ 5 cours Saint-Louis ☎ 04 91 33 14 94 🕐 Closed Tue evening & all day Sun 🚌 Bus 31,33,34,41,80,81

Ste-Maries-de-la-Mer

Chante-Clair (££)

The best seafood in town, weighed and grilled on the spot. Try the *tellines Camarguais* (▶ 36/37).

✉ place des Remparts ☎ 04 90 97 82 95 🕐 Open Easter–Nov. Closed Tue except Jul & Aug

St-Rémy-de-Provence

Café des Arts (£)

Join the locals in St-Rémy's most popular restaurant, with its steak and frogs' legs specialities.

✉ 30 boulevard Victor Hugo ☎ 04 90 92 08 50 🕐 Closed Wed & Nov–Mar

Lou Planet (£)

The tasty crêpes, galettes, salads and ice-creams here make ideal lunch snacks.

✉ 7 Place Favier ☎ 04 90 92 19 81

Bouillabaisse

This world-famous fish soup originated in Marseille as a nourishing family meal, made with choice fish kept aside by the fishermen especially for their families. It is traditionally made with up to a dozen different kinds of fish, cooked in a stock containing saffron, herbs and fennel. It is served with croûtons, which are smeared with *rouille* (a sauce of fresh red chilli peppers crushed with garlic and olive oil), sprinkled with cheese then dunked in the soup.

Var & Haute-Provence

Alain Ducasse

Don't expect to find Monsieur Ducasse himself in the kitchen here as he is far too busy looking after his new restaurant in Paris, having recently left the famous Louis XV in Monaco (▶ 98). Instead he has entrusted the cooking to star pupil, Monegasque Sonia Lee, who delights her guests with sensational dishes which embrace all the flavours and perfumes of Haute Provence.

Bormes-les-Mimosas

L'Escoundudo (££)

Enjoy wholesome regional dishes flavoured with herbs from the surrounding hills, on a sunny terrace brimming with bougainvillea, hidden in a steep back alley.

✉ 4 ruelle du Moulin ☎ 04 94 71 15 53 🕐 Closed Sat & Sun out of season

Le Jardin de Perlefleurs (£££)

Borme's top eatery. It is difficult to better Guy Gedda's exquisite *soupe au pistou*, rabbit tart and Provençal *daube*.

✉ 100 chemin de l'Orangerie ☎ 04 94 64 99 23 🕐 Evenings only. Closed Mon

Briançon

Gouli du Temple (£)

Specialities and *charcuteries* from the mountains.

✉ 5 place du Temple ☎ 04 92 20 43 26 🕐 May–Sep (delicatessen only Oct–Apr)

Cogolin

Port-Diffa (££)

One of Provence's top Moroccan restaurants.

✉ Le Pont sur la giscle (RN98 – La Foux) ☎ 04 94 56 29 07 🕐 Open Mar–Jan. Closed Mon

Collobrières

La Petite Fontaine (£)

Try some local delicacies of the Massif des Maures, washed down with wine from the local cooperative on a shady terrace. Peaceful.

✉ 1 place de la République ☎ 04 94 48 00 12 🕐 Closed Sun evening & Mon

Digne-Les-Bains

Le Grand Paris (££)

With the reputaion of Digne's best restaurant, and situated in a former 17th-century convent. Try the pigeon accompanied by courgette flowers cooked in the juice of truffles.

✉ 19 boulevard Thiers ☎ 04 92 31 11 15 🕐 Closed Sun evening, Mon, 21 Dec–1 Mar

Fayence

Le Castelleras (£££)

Frogs legs wrapped in pastry with cream and chives is one of many local specialities served in this old stone *mas*.

✉ Route de Seillans ☎ 04 94 76 13 80 🕐 Closed Wed

Frejus

Brasserie des Arenes (£)

This unlikely-looking café near the Arena offers tasty, filling portions of *entrecôte frites* or *moules frites* for under F60.

✉ Rondpoint les Arenes ☎ 04 94 51 41 55

Gap

Le Tourton Des Alpes (££)

The local speciality of *tourtons* – tiny hot pastry envelopes filled with either potato, spinach, meat, prune or apple – are served here in copious quantities.

✉ 1 rue des Cordiers ☎ 04 92 53 90 91

La Grande-Freinet

Auberge Sarrasin (££)

This cosy, intimate restaurant at the heart of the Massif des Maures provides the perfect venue to taste *cassoulet Provençal* (a hotpot of white beans, pork and white wine) by the log fire in winter.

✉ D558, Massif des Maures ☎ 04 94 43 67 16 🕐 Closed Mon.

Grimaud
Les Santons (££)
Classic cuisine and impeccable service in elegant Provençal surroundings. One of the region's top restaurants.
✉ Route Nationale ☎ 04 94 43 21 02 🕐 Closed Wed & Nov–mid-Mar

Hyères
La Bergerie (£)
Tasty salads, *crêpes* and pizzas followed by homemade ice cream in casual, friendly surroundings.
✉ 16 rue de Limans ☎ 04 94 65 57 97 🕐 Closed Sat & Sun lunch. Also Sun evening out of season

Les Issambres
Villa Saint-Elme (£££)
One of the coast's most spectacular restaurant terraces, with exceptional cuisine to match. Try the lobster tart followed by *pigeon en croûte*.
✉ Corniche des Issambres ☎ 04 94 49 52 52 🕐 Closed Wed (Oct–Jan) & Jan–end Mar

Miramar
La Marine (££)
Possibly the best sardines on the Corniche d'Or, on a breezy terrace overhanging the Mediterranean.
✉ Port de Miramar ☎ No telephone 🕐 Closed out of season

Moustiers-Ste-Marie
La Bastide de Moustiers (££)
Dine in the country home of the world's top chef, Alain Ducasse. Surprisingly affordable (▶ panel).
✉ 04360 La Grisolière ☎ 04 92 70 47 47 🕐 Closed Jan–mid-Mar

Les Santons (££)
Widespread reputation for good food and a pretty setting.
✉ place de l'Église ☎ 04 92 74 66 48 🕐 Closed Mon lunchtime, Tue, Dec & Jan

Sisteron
Hotel Restaurant de la Citadelle (££)
Enjoy a spectacular alpine panorama whilst trying local delicacies *fougasse à l'anchois* (anchovy stuffed bread) or Sisteron lamb with thyme and rosemary.
✉ 126 rue Saunerie ☎ 04 92 61 13 52

St Tropez
Le Bar à Vin (££)
A cosy bistro, hidden in a quiet back street and highly recommended by locals.
✉ 13 rue des Feniers ☎ 04 94 97 46 10 🕐 evenings only. Closed 7 Jan–15 Feb, Wed until 15 Apr

La Bouillabaisse (££)
A speciality fish restaurant in an ancient fisherman's cottage on the beach. Plenty of atmosphere.
✉ Plage de la Bouillabaisse ☎ 04 94 97 54 00 🕐 Closed mid-Jan–mid-Feb, mid-Nov–mid-Dec

La Brasserie Asiatique (££)
The exotic oriental dishes here make a pleasant change from Provençal cuisine.
✉ Résidence du Port ☎ 04 94 97 84 82

La Citadelle (££)
This tiny atmospheric restaurant spills out on to the street. Don't miss the tarte tatin.
✉ 22 bis rue de la Citadelle ☎ 04 94 54 81 19 🕐 Apr–mid-Oct dinner only. Also lunch from Apr–mid Jun

'In' with the Jet Set
Tips on where to be seen and when during your stay in St Tropez.... For breakfast, Sénéquier's Salon de Thé (✉ quai de Suffren) is a must. *Boules* is on the lunchtime menu at Café des Arts, Place des Lices' number one address. L'Echalote (✉ 35 rue Allard) is currently 'in' for dinner, and the notorious Tropezien institution, Le Gorille (✉ quai de Suffren) remains the place to eat steak tartare after nightclubs close at dawn.

Alpes-Maritimes

Nice's Top Chef
Irresistable local dishes such as *pate au pistou* and *tripes Niçoise* are the trademarks of Dominic Le Stanc, until recently chef of the Negresco's famous Chantecler restaurant, and a name synonymous with the very best in Provençal cuisine. Now all eyes are on La Mérenda, newly acquired by Le Stanc – a tiny rustic restaurant already popular among Niçois gourmets.

Antibes
Le Bacon (£££)
One of the coast's best fish restaurants, with exceptional views over old Antibes.
✉ **boulevard Bacon, Cap d'Antibes** ☎ **04 93 61 50 92**
🕐 **Closed Mon (except Jul & Aug) & Nov–Jan**

Biot
Auberge du Jarrier (££)
Imaginative cuisine and an unmistakably Provençal flavour in an old jar factory.
✉ **30 passage de la Bourgade** ☎ **04 93 65 53 48** 🕐 **Closed Wed evening**

Cannes
Le Croco (£)
Be sure to try the speciality barbecued fish and meat *brochettes* (kebabs), followed by *crème brûlée* in this popular, friendly bistro.
✉ **11 rue Louis-Blanc** ☎ **04 93 68 60 55** 🕐 **Closed Sun**

L'Espadon (£)
Take refuge from the glitz and glamour of Cannes in this cheap, cheerful, no-frills fish restaurant by the old port. Delicious paella.
✉ **9 quai St Pierre** ☎ **no telephone**

La Palme d'Or (£££)
Join the stars at Cannes' most prestigious restaurant, to experience some of prize-winning Master Chef Christian Willer's latest culinary creations.
✉ **Hotel Martinez** ☎ **04 92 98 74 14** 🕐 **Closed Mon & Tue out of season**

Èze
La Bergerie (££)
Traditional dishes with a good choice of Côtes-de-Provence wines. Winter by the open fire, summer on the shady terrace overlooking the sea.
✉ **RN7, Èze** ☎ **04 93 41 03 67**
🕐 **Closed Mon–Wed evening**

La Chèvre D'or (£££)
Breathtaking sea views and inspired French cuisine.
✉ **3 rue du Barri** ☎ **04 92 10 66 66** 🕐 **Closed mid-Nov–Feb**

Juan-Les-Pins
L'Oasis (££)
Dine on the beach at this restaurant, with views sweeping from the Cap d'Antibes to the Îles Lérins.
✉ **Blvd Charles Guilaumont** ☎ **04 93 61 45 15** 🕐 **Closed eveings in winter**

Menton
Don Cicco (£)
Italian cuisine just one kilometre from the Italian border.
✉ **11 rue St-Michel** ☎ **04 93 57 92 92**

La Nautique (£)
Highly recommended for fish-lovers.
✉ **27 Quai de MonléoN** ☎ **04 93 90 03 47**

Monaco
Louis XV (£££)
Should you break the bank at the Casino, come to the Louis XV, with its three Michelin rosettes, to blow your winnings.
✉ **Hotel de Paris, place du Casino** ☎ **04 92 16 30 01**
🕐 **Closed Tue, Wed lunchtime**

Mougins
Le Moulin de Mougins (£££)
World-famous chef Roger Vergé invented the phrase 'cuisine of the sun' to describe his *nouvelle*

Provençal cookery.

✉ Notre-Dame de Vie ☎ 04 93 75 78 24 🕐 Closed Mon, Thu lunchtime

Mougins

Relais à Mougins (£££)

Another of Mougin's gastronomic bastions. Master chef André Surmain's is well-known for his seasonal cuisine.

✉ Place de la Mairie ☎ 04 93 90 03 47 🕐 Closed Mon & Tue lunch in winter

Nice

Auberge des Arts (££)

The imaginative culinary creations of young chef David Faure are a seductive blend of classic French and Nissart cuisine. His delectable desserts are works of art.

✉ 9 rue Pairolière ☎ 04 93 85 63 53 🕐 Closed Sun evening & Mon 🚌 all buses

Chantecler (£££)

Nice's leading restaurant – a bastion of French gastronomy.

✉ Hôtel Negresco, 37, promenade des Anglais ☎ 04 93 88 39 51 🕐 15 Nov–15 Dec 🚌 buses 6,11

Fenocchio (£)

The best ice creams on the Côte d'Azur.

✉ Place Rossetti ☎ 04 93 80 72 52 🕐 daily 10am–midnight 🚌 all buses

Flo (££)

Brasserie-style restaurant in a converted *art deco* theatre with the kitchen on stage! Special late night menu up to half past midnight.

✉ 4 rue Sacha Guitry ☎ 04 93 13 38 38 🕐 daily, lunch & dinner. 🚌 1, 2, 4, 5, 9, 10, 14, 22, 23, 24

Lou Pilha Leva (£)

Niçois fast-food (▶ panel).

✉ 10 rue du Collet ☎ 04 93 13 99 08 🕐 10–10 (midnight in summer) 🚌 all buses

La Mérenda (££)

Irresistable menu of Nissart specialities, lovingly prepared by one of France's most outstanding chefs (▶ panel).

✉ 4 rue de la Terrace ☎ No telephone 🕐 Closed weekends & hols. 🚌 all buses ❓ Credit cards not accepted

La Petite Maison (££)

Local market-fresh dishes near the Opèra. The *hors-d'oeuvres Niçois* is a meal in itself. Book well in advance.

✉ 11 rue St-François-de-Paule ☎ 04 93 92 59 59 🕐 Closed Sun 🚌 all buses

La Rotonde (£)

The Riviera's most original brasserie. Bright merry-go-round décor, complete with flashing lights, automats and painted wooden horses.

✉ Hôtel Negresco, 37 promenade des Anglais ☎ 04 93 16 64 00 🕐 7am–midnight 🚌 buses 6, 11

Le Transsiberien (££)

An epic culinary journey of authentic bortsch and blinis in a great Trans-Siberian rail-carriage.

✉ 1 rue Bottero ☎ 04 93 96 49 05 🕐 Closed Sun evening & all day Mon. 🚌 bus 6, 7, 9, 10, 12, 23, 24, 26

Saint-Paul-de-Vence

Mas d'Artigny (£££)

Well-known for its *fruits de mer* and fish dishes. Not cheap but worth every franc.

✉ Route de la Colle ☎ 04 93 32 84 54

Lou Pilha Leva

'Lou Pilha Leva' in local Nissart patois means 'you take away'. At the heart of old Nice, this hole-in-the-wall serves piping hot plates of socca, pissaladière, beignets, farcis, pizza and other Niçois specialities (▶ 36–7) – F40 will buy you a bit of everything! Ideal for a snack lunch, the trestle tables provide the perfect opportunity to chat to the locals.

Vaucluse

Île de Barthelasse
This island on the Rhône has a colourful and varied history. Once a hunting reserve, it then became the gathering-place of Avignonais prostitutes and thieves, but in later years it was a fashionable place to promenade and picnic. Today it is still a popular recreation site with a lovely open-air swimming pool, camp sites and several *chambres d'hôtes*.

Prices
Expect to pay the following per night:

£ = up to F250
££ = up to F400
£££ = over F400

Apt
Auberge du Lubéron (££)
Apt's top hotel, beside the river.
✉ **17 quai Léon Sagy** ☎ **04 90 74 12 50**

Avignon
Auberge de Cassagne (£££)
Ancient Provençal dwelling five minutes from Avignon, with beautiful gardens, outdoor pool and a gastonomic restaurant of international renown.
✉ **450 allée de Cassagne, Le Pontet** ☎ **04 90 31 04 18**

La Ferme (£)
Old farmhouse on the Île du Barthelasse (▶ panel). The twee gypsy caravans in the garden are popular with actors during the summer festival.
✉ **Chemin des Bois, Île de la Barthelasse** ☎ **04 90 82 57 53**
🕐 **Closed Jan**

La Mirande (£££)
Refined, elegant hotel set in a medieval cardinal's palace in a tranquil cobbled square at the foot of the Popes' Palace.
✉ **4 place de la Mirande** ☎ **04 90 85 93 93**

Bonnieux
De l'Aiguebrun (££)
A beautiful old, stone farmhouse 6km east of Bonnieux, peacefully located at the heart of the Lúberon National Park.
✉ **Relais de la Canube** ☎ **04 90 74 01 14**

Gordes
Les Bories (£££)
Luxury hillside hotel with tennis court and an elegant marble indoor pool. The restaurant is in a restored stone *borie*.
✉ **route de l'Abbaye de Sénanque** ☎ **04 90 72 00 51**

Lacoste
Relais du Procurer (£££)
Luxury B&B in the midst of a chic village.
✉ **rue Basse** ☎ **04 90 75 82 28**

Lourmarin
Hostellerie le Paradou (££)
Small, sleepy hotel, beneath the gorges of Lourmarin.
✉ **Combe de Lourmarin, (D943)** ☎ **04 90 68 04 05**

Orange
Arène (££)
Small 3-star hotel in quiet traffic-free square in the historic town centre.
✉ **Place de Langes** ☎ **04 90 11 40 40**

Roussillon
Mamaison (££)
Small old farmhouse with rooms decorated by local artists and a restaurant which specialises in home-grown organic vegetarian dishes.
✉ **Quartier Les Devens** ☎ **04 90 05 74 17**

Vaison-la-Romaine
Hostellerie le Beffroi (££)
Atmospheric 'olde-worlde' hotel in Vaison's ancient *haute ville*.
✉ **2 place Monfort** ☎ **04 90 36 04 71**

Venasque
La Maison Aux Volets Bleus (££)
A quaint B&B overlooking the Vaucluse hills, with five rooms attractively decorated with dried flowers and Provençal prints. Closed in winter.
✉ **84210 Venasque** ☎ **04 90 66 03 04**

Bouches-du-Rhône

Aix
Des Augustins (£££)
Intriguing blend of history and modernity within a 15th-century former Augustine convent.

✉ 3 rue de la Masse ☎ 04 42 27 28 59 🕐 Closed mid-Jan–mid-Feb

Le Pigonnet (£££)
Beautiful family-run *bastide* hotel with antique furniture, rose arbours and views over the countryside.

✉ 5 avenue du Pigonnet ☎ 04 42 59 02 90

Arles
Calendal (££)
Stylish Provençal mansion. Some rooms overlook the Roman arena.

✉ 23 place du Docteur Pomme ☎ 04 90 96 11 89

Hôtel d'Arlatan
This charming 16th century residence of the Comtes d'Arlatan is one of the region's most beautiful historic hotels, with 30 rooms individually decorated with Provençal antiques.

✉ 26 rue Sauvage ☎ 04 90 93 56 66

Nord-Pinus (£££)
Unique hotel and a classified national monument. The Nord-Pinus is a hotel of strong literary connections, once a favourite haunt of the Félibres poets, and other literati, including Stendhal, Mistral, Cocteau and Henry James. Today it is popular with Christian Lacroix, top matadors and other wealthy aficionados, and is decorated accordingly with bullfighting posters, trophies and the mounted heads of unfortunate bulls. Without doubt the place for people who want to feel truly Arlésien!

✉ place du Forum ☎ 04 90 93 44 44 🕐 Closed Jan–Mar

St-Pierre les Aubagne
Hostellerie de la Source (££)
Small 3-star hotel near Aubagne. Garden, pool and tennis court.

☎ 04 42 04 09 19

Fontvieille
Auberge de la Régalido (£££)
Warm, friendly auberge in a converted oil-mill.

✉ rue Frédéric-Mistral ☎ 04 90 54 60 22 🕐 Closed Jan & early Feb

Marseille
Le Corbusier (£)
Part of an avant-garde experiment in architectural design by Le Corbusier (▶ panel).

✉ 280 boulevard Michelet, 8e. ☎ 04 91 16 78 00 🚌 Bus 21, 21S, 22, 22S

Mercure Beauvau Vieux-Port (£££)
Overlooking the port and often used as a backdrop in films. Past guests include Chopin, George Sand, Cocteau and Hemmingway.

✉ 4 rue Beauvau, 13001 Marseille ☎ 04 91 54 91 00 🚇 Metro 1 (Vieux Port)

St-Rémy-de-Provence
Villa Glanum (£)
Simple hotel near Glanum with a swimming-pool and horses.

✉ 46 avenue Van Gogh ☎ 04 90 92 03 59 🕐 Closed Jan

Ste-Maries-de-la-Mer
Hostellerie de Cacharel (££)
A former *gardian* ranch in the heart of the marshes. Horse riding and bull-watching.

✉ route de Cacharel ☎ 04 90 97 95 44

La Cité Radieuse
In 1952 Le Corbusier built a massive 17-storey concrete building intended to be part of a 6-block *Cité Radieuse* (Radiant City), designed as a prototype for 'vertical living', combining living space, shops, schools and recreational facilities all under one roof. Sadly it looks far from radiant and the Marseillais soon dubbed it the 'madman's house'.

Var & Haute-Provence

Great Views
A medieval fortress perched on a hill, Château de Trigance has lots of atmosphere and a superb outlook. It is above the village of Trigance, but the views are for miles.
(☎ 04 94 76 91 18)

Anthéor – Cap-Roux
Auberge d'Anthéor (£££)
A tiny, modern hotel, halfway along the Corniche d'Or. Although there is no beach, there is a small dock for swimming and a pool.
✉ N98, Anthéor ☎ 04 94 44 83 38

Bormes les Mimosas
Le Bellevue (£)
A simple *Logis de France* with spectacular views over red roofs to the sparkling sea.
✉ 12 place Gambetta ☎ 04 94 71 15 15 ◷ Closed winter

Cogolin
Au Coq Hôtel (££)
This cheerful pink hotel, at the bustling heart of Cogolin, offers affordable accommodation for those wishing to worship the Tropezienne sun without paying St Tropez prices.
✉ Place de la République ☎ 04 95 54 63 14

Cotignac
Lou Calen
A stylish Varois town house, decorated with rustic antique furniture. Beautiful shady garden and swimming-pool.
✉ 1 Cours Gambetta ☎ 04 94 04 60 40

Forcalquier
Hostellerie des Deux Lions (££)
Charming old coaching-inn with rustic décor and delicious local dishes.
✉ 11 place du Bourguet ☎ 04 92 75 25 30

Gorges du Verdon
Hôtel-Restaurant du Grand Canyon (£££)
Stay here for a room with a view.

✉ Falaise des Cavaliers, D71, Aiguines ☎ 04 94 76 91 31

Gréoux-les-Bains
Villa Borghese (££)
A delightful hotel with flower-filled balconies, charming garden and pool.
✉ avenue des Thermes ☎ 04 92 78 00 91 ◷ Closed Dec–Mar

Monetier-les-Bains
L'Auberge du Choucas (££)
Cosy farmhouse high in the Alps, and ideal for skiing at Serre Chevalier.
✉ Monetier-Les-Bains, 14km N of Briançon ☎ 04 92 24 42 73 ◷ Closed Nov–mid-Dec

Moustiers-Ste-Marie
Bonne Auberge (£)
Clean, modest hotel near the great Verdon gorges. Popular with walkers.
✉ route de Castellane ☎ 04 92 74 66 18

St Tropez
Château de la Messardiere (£££)
St Tropez's most luxurious hotel. Truly palatial.
✉ route de Tahiti ☎ 04 94 56 76 00

Mas de Chastelas (£££)
Stay with Depardieu, Belmondo and other French film idols at this beautiful 18th-century *mas*, surrounded by vineyards just outside St Tropez.
✉ Quartier Bertaud, Gassin ☎ 04 94 56 71 71

St Véran
Les Chalets du Villard (££)
Traditional Alpine chalet accommodation in the highest village in Europe.
✉ 05350 Saint-Véran ☎ 04 92 45 82 08

Alpes-Maritimes

Cannes
Martinez (£££)
This deluxe hotel contains Cannes' top restaurant, La Palm d'Or – excellent for star-spotting during the Film Festival

✉ 73 La Croisette ☎ 04 92 98 73 00

Cap D'Antibes
Hotel du Cap Eden Roc (£££)
'A large, proud, rose-coloured hotel. Deferential palms cool its flushed façade, and before it stretches a ... bright tan prayer rug of a beach.'
(F Scott Fitzgerald *Tender is the Night*)

✉ boulevard Kennedy ☎ 04 93 61 39 01 ⏱ Open mid-Apr–mid-Oct

Èze
Château Èza (£££)
A stunning collection of medieval houses, linked together to form a luxury eagle's nest.

✉ rue de la Pise ☎ 04 93 41 12 24

Menton
Le Mondial (££)
Old-fashioned, turn-of-the-century hotel with a cafeteria-style restaurant. Excellent value and extremely popular all year round.

✉ 12 rue Partouneaux ☎ 04 92 10 20 66

Monaco
Hôtel de Paris (£££)
Monte Carlo's most prestigious address.

✉ place du Casino ☎ 04 92 16 30 00

Nice
Château des Ollières (£££)
Exclusive *Belle Époque* villa, once owned by a Russian prince.

✉ 39 avenue des Baumettes ☎ 04 92 15 77 99 🚌 bus 6, 9, 10, 12, 23, 24, 26

Negresco (£££)
World-famous hotel built in the *Belle Époque* style.

✉ 37 promenade des Anglais ☎ 04 93 16 64 00 🚌 bus 6, 7, 9, 10, 12, airport bus

Palais Maeterlinck (£££)
Once the home of poet Maurice Maeterlinck, now a palatial, modern coastal hotel.

✉ 30 boulevard Maurice Maeterlinck ☎ 04 92 00 72 00 ⏱ Closed early Jan–mid-Mar 🚌 bus 14

Primotel Suisse (££)
An affordable address on the water front.

✉ 15 quai Raubà Capéu ☎ 04 92 17 39 00 🚌 bus 38

Solara (£)
Excellent value in Nice's chic pedestrian zone.

✉ 7 rue de France ☎ 04 93 88 09 96

St Paul de Vence
Hotel Colomb d'Or (£££)
Once a modest 1920s café where Braque, Matisse, Picasso and Léger paid for their drinks with canvases. Now a deluxe hotel.

✉ place du Général de Gaulle ☎ 04 93 32 80 02

St-Jean-Cap-Ferrat
Grand Hotel du Cap Ferrat (£££)
Sumptuous palace, in lush, tropical gardens, amidst some of the world's most expensive real estate.

✉ Blvd Géneral de Gaulle ☎ 04 93 76 13 02

Famous Guests
Charlie Chaplin taught his children to swim in the pool of the Grand Hôtel du Cap Ferrat. Queen Victoria was one of the first famous residents of the Hôtel de Paris; Michael Jackson one of the more recent.

Provençal Souvenirs & Gifts

Opening Times
Most shops in Provence and the Côte d'Azur are open from Tuesday to Saturday between 8 or 10–12 and 2–6 although some stay open longer at the height of the summer season or during festival times.

A Ray of Sunshine
Souleiado is a Provençal word meaning 'a sun-ray piercing through the clouds' and is the name of the leading manufacturer of block-printed Provençal textiles. The company was founded in 1938 by Charles Deméry in a successful attempt to revive a 200 year-old textile industry in Tarascon. The Musée Souleiado (⊠ 39 rue Proudhon, Tarascon ☎ 04 90 91 08 80 ⊙ open by appointment only) includes 40,000 18th-century fruitwood blocks which are still the basis for all the Souleiado patterns today.

Vaucluse

Avignon
Souleiado
Colour-drenched printed fabrics, traditional Provençal clothing and gifts ideas.
⊠ 5 rue Joseph Vernet ☎ 04 90 86 47 67

Bouches-du-Rhône

Arles
L'Arlésienne
Traditional Camarguais costumes.
⊠ 12 rue du Président Wilson ☎ 04 90 93 28 05

Bijouterie Pinus
Necklaces, bracelets and crosses in traditional Provençal designs.
⊠ 6 rue Jean Jaurès ☎ 04 90 96 04 63

Aubagne
Atelier Louis Sicard
Manufacturer of *faïence* and *santons* (small terracotta figures dressed or painted in regional costumes) in Aubagne, the pottery capital of France.
⊠ 2 boulevard Emile Combes ☎ 04 42 70 12 92

Marseille
La Compagnie de Provence
One of Marseille's few remaining specialist soap shops.
⊠ 1 rue Caisserie, 13218 Marseille ☎ 04 91 56 20 94 Ⓜ Metro 1 (Vieux Port)

St-Rémy-de-Provence
Santoline
Ça sent la Provence! Apple blossom mingled with jasmine, rose with mimosa to create an intoxicating blend of pot pourris.
⊠ 34 avenue Victor Hugo ☎ 04 90 92 11 96 ⊙ Variable opening hours in winter.

Var and Haute-Provence

Digne
La Maison de laLavande
Every imaginable lavender product is here – *even* lavender liqueur.
⊠ 34 boulevard Gassendi ☎ 04 92 31 33 94

St Tropez
Pierre Basset
Terracotta and enameled tiles, jars, pots and vases in sunny colours.
⊠ route des Plages ☎ 04 94 97 75 06

Alpes-Maritimes

Biot
Verrerie de Biot
Traditional bubble-flecked glassware from Provence's capital of glass-blowing makes an unusual souvenir or gift.
⊠ Chemin des Combes ☎ 04 93 65 03 00

Grasse
Parfumerie Fragonard
The very finest perfumes from Provence. Interesting guided tours.
⊠ 20 blvd Fragonard ☎ 04 93 36 44 65

Nice
Parfums Poilpot
Tiny, traditional perfumerie with a wide choice of scents from Grasse.
⊠ 10 rue St-Gaëtan ☎ 04 93 85 60 77 🚌 all buses

Fashion

Vaucluse

Avignon
Alain Manoukian
Chic, affordable women's clothing by a local designer.
✉ **11 rue Joseph Vernet**
☎ **04 90 82 42 52**

La Boutique du Sac
Buy an extra bag for all your souvenirs.
✉ **17 rue de la République**
☎ **04 90 82 08 50**

Mouret Chapelier
One of France's few remaining traditional milliners.
✉ **20 rue des Marchands**
☎ **04 90 85 39 38**

Bouches-du-Rhône

Aix
Jules & Jim
Gant, Timberland, Calvin Klein, Armani and other trendy fashions for men.
✉ **67 Cours Mirabeau** ☎ **04 42 93 55 20**

Petit Lune
Enchanting children's fashions from 0–8 years.
✉ **11 rue Aude** ☎ **04 42 27 30 01**

Arles
Christian Lacroix
The boutique of the world-famous Arles-born designer (see panel).
✉ **52 rue de la République**
☎ **04 90 96 11 16**

Gallia
Smart shoes in a beautifully-restored 12th-century monastery.
✉ **38 rue de la République**
☎ **04 90 96 10 36**

Marseille
Noir C'est Noir
Young, trendy fashions by Marseille designer, Dominique Ghré.
✉ **65 rue Paradis** ☎ **04 91 33 61 15** 🚇 **Métro 1 (Vieux Port)**

Var and Haute-Provence

Gap
Technicien du Sport
The latest fashions in ski clothing and equipment.
✉ **39 rue St Arey** ☎ **04 92 53 95 21**

St Tropez
Blanc Bleu
Stylish, sporty fashion for both sexes.
✉ **3 rue Allard** ☎ **04 94 97 08 01**

Hermès
The ultimate in French chic.
✉ **2 rue de la Mesange** ☎ **04 88 32 39 91**

Alpes-Maritimes

Biot
Chacok
Bright colours and bold designs by Biot designer Arlette Chacok in Biot.
✉ **route de la Mer, Biot**
☎ **04 93 65 60 60**

Cannes
Cravatterie Nazionali
Designer ties.
✉ **79 rue d'Antibes** ☎ **04 93 99 78 88**

Nice
Durrani
Classic haute couture and exclusive perfumes, created by the King of Afghanistan!
✉ **8 rue Massenet, Nice**
☎ **04 93 87 26 34**

Local Genius
Christian Lacroix was born in Arles under the star sign of Taurus, the symbol of Camargue. One of haute-couture's most innovative and eclectic designers, his clothes are classic yet daring, feminine yet boldly Mediterranean, frequently inspired by the traditional Arlésian costumes. The fashions, jewellery, hats and handbags of his flamboyant boutique at the very heart of Arles' pedestrian zone represent a fashion mecca for the rich and fashionable.

Food & Drink

Too Many Sweets Give You Tooth 'Aix!

The traditional souvenirs of Aix are its *calissons*, delicious almond and melon sweets first created in 1473 and still made in the old-fashioned way by mixing ground almonds with glazed melons and fruit syrup. Beautifully packaged and best bought from Béchard, Riederer (✉ 6 rue Thiers) or Roy René (✉ rue Papassaudi), they make excellent presents... if you can resist eating them all yourself.

Vaucluse

Apt
Aptunion
Apt claims to be the world leader in crystallised fruits and this is the top shop in town. Phone in advance for a factory tour.
✉ **N100 (direction Avignon)** ☎ **04 90 74 65 64**

Avignon
J M Blanes
A traditional sweetshop selling local herb-liqueur *Papalines d'Avignon* truffles, *Palais des Papes* caramels and apricot-filled *Rochers des Domes* pralines.
✉ **20 rue St Agricol** ☎ **04 90 82 32 93**

Les Halles
This modern, covered farmers market is the perfect place to buy for a picnic.
✉ **Place Pie** 🕐 **Tue–Sun 6AM–1PM**

Carpentras
R Clavel
This fifth generation sweet shop claims the world record for making the largest *berlingot* candy.
✉ **Place Pie** 🕐 **Tue–Sun 6AM–1PM**

L'Isle-Sur-La-Sorgue
Les Délices du Lubéron
A tasty selection of olive oil, *tapenades*, herbs, nougats, candies and other regional products.
✉ **270 avenue Voltaire-Garcin** ☎ **04 90 38 45 96**

Vaison-La-Romaine
Lanchier-Avias
Traditional - style biscuits and pastries.
✉ **Place Montet** ☎ **04 90 36 09 25**

Lou Canesteou
Vaison's best cheese shop offers a wide choice of locally-made *chèvre* including *banon* (wrapped in oak leaves), *picadon* and *cachat*.
✉ **10 rue Raspail** ☎ **04 90 36 31 30**

Bouches-du-Rhône

Mouriès
Moulin à Huile Coopératif
This unlikely looking shed sells some of the best olive oil in France.
✉ **Off D17 (direction Eyguières)** ☎ **04 90 47 50 01** 🕐 **Open Wed 2–6, Sat 8.30–12, 2–6**

Aix
Chocolaterie Puyricard
Puyricard's hand-made chocolates are considered the finest in France. Visit their traditional chocolate factory in a northern suburb.
✉ **Quartier Beaufort, Puyricard** ☎ **04 42 96 11 21**

Maison Béchard
An old-fashioned sweetshop, well-known for its *calissons*
✉ **12 cours Mirabeau** ☎ **04 42 26 06 78**

Richart
Sophisticated designer chocolates.
✉ **8 rue Thiers** ☎ **04 42 38 16 19**

Arles
Pierre milhau
An old-fashioned *charcuterie*. Famous Arles' sausages, Camargue sausages, bull sausages. Rumour has it they even make donkey sausages!
✉ **11 rue Réattu** ☎ **04 90 96 16 05**

Aubagne
Distillerie Janot
Tastings of *Pastis*, Provence's most popular liqueur. Visits by appointment only.
✉ **avenue du Pastre, ZI les Paluds** ☎ **04 42 82 29 57**

Marseille
Le Four des Navettes
Marseille's oldest bakery. Try the famous orange-flower *navette* biscuits, in the shape of the Sainte-Maries' legendary boat (► 57), originally only made for the Catholic feast day of Candlemas.
✉ **136 rue Sainte** ☎ **04 91 33 32 12** 🚌 **Bus 55, 61, 81**

Torrefaction Rioailles
Mouth-watering sweet-shop-cum-tea salon.
✉ **56 La Canebière** ☎ **04 91 55 60 66** 🚇 **Métro 2 (Noailles)**

Var and Haute-Provence

Gap
Les 4 Saisons
Delicious mountain produce – fruit, vegetables, cheeses, truffles, pâtés, honey and herbs.
✉ **place aux Herbes** ☎ **04 92 53 63 42**

St Tropez (Gassin)
Petit Village
Wines of the Mâitres Vignerons of St Tropez.
✉ **La Foux, Gassin** ☎ **04 94 56 32 04**

Alpes-Maritimes

Cannes
Ceneri
One of France's top cheese stores with over 300 different types, from huge rounds of runny brie to tiny *boutons de culotte* (trouser-button) goats' cheese.
✉ **22 rue Meynadier** ☎ **04 93 43 07 70**

Mougins
Boutique du Moulin
If you can't afford dinner in one of France's top establishments (► 98), console yourself with a mustard, jam or *tapenade* from chef Roger Vergés shop.
✉ **place du Commandant Lamy** ☎ **04 93 90 00 91**

Nice
Alziari
This old family shop presses their own olive oil and sells *olives de Nice* by the kilo. A veritable Niçois institution.
✉ **14 rue Saint-François-de-Paule** ☎ **04 93 85 76 92** 🚌 **all buses**

Caprioglio
Wine store in old Nice, to suit all purses from *vin de table* (stored in giant orange tanks) to the top *crus*.
✉ **16 rue de la Préfecture** ☎ **04 93 85 66 57** 🚌 **all buses**

Espuno
One of France's best bakeries. Try the regional *fougasse*.
✉ **35 rue Droite** ☎ **04 93 80 50 67** 🚌 **all buses**

Maison Auer
Nice's last traditional maker of crystallised fruits, famed throughout France.
✉ **7 rue St François de Paule** ☎ **04 93 85 77 98** 🚌 **all buses**

The Art of Drinking 'Pastis'
Ice cubes first, then *pastis*, then water – a hallowed trio for a great Provençal custom – the *apéritif*. There are many different ways to drink pastis – *noyé* (drowned) with lots of water, *en flanc*, thick and strong, with very little water or as a cocktail: Try the 'parrot' (with mint syrup), the 'tomato' (with grenadine) or the 'Moorish' (with a bitter almond syrup). *Santé*!

Art & Antiques

Books for Tea
Avignon booksellers certainly know how best to sell their books, accompanied by a good cup of tea and a pâtisserie! There's nothing more enjoyable than browsing through your newly-purchased book on Provence over scones and cream on the sun-drenched patio of Shakespeare.
Alternatively, try Les Félibres (✉ 14–16 rue du Limas
☎ 04 90 27 39 05) a specialist interior design, gardening and cookery bookshop. According to locals, they serve the best pastries in town!

Vaucluse

Avignon
Hervé Baum
Modern and antique, chic and rustic – objects for home and garden.
✉ 19 rue Petite Fusterie
☎ 04 90 86 37 66

Le Peinturluron
A painter's paradise, in case you feel inspired by the Provençal scenery.
✉ 72 rue de la Bonneterie
☎ 04 90 85 37 16

Shakespeare
A discount English bookshop and tea shop. Occasional readings and recitals too. (► panel).
✉ 155 rue Carreterie ☎ 04 90 27 38 50

L'Isle-Sur-La-Sorgue
L'Isle aux Brocantes
There are over 35 dealers here, trading in an 'antique village' atmosphere.
✉ Passage du Pont, 7 Avenue des 4 Otages ☎ 04 90 20 69 93

Roussillon
Galerie des Ocres
Gifts and paints in every imaginable shade of ochre from Europe's 'Grand Canyon' (► 24/5).
✉ Le Castrum ☎ 04 90 05 62 99

Bouches-du-Rhône

Aix
Librairie de Provence
Large bookshop with an excellent choice of regional travel, literature and culinary titles.
✉ 31 Cours Mirabeau ☎ 04 42 26 07 23

Yves Ungaro
An aladdin's cave of pictures and objects d'art at the heart of Aix's antiques quarter.
✉ 1 rue Jaubert ☎ 04 42 63 10 33

Arles
Antiquités Maurin
A treasure trove of regional furniture, paintings and ceramics from the 17th to the 20th century. Worldwide shipping service available.
✉ 4 rue de Grille ☎ 04 90 93 69 00

Librairie Actes Sud
Bookshop of Arles' world famous Actes Sud publishing house, located in Le Méjan, a lively arts complex with a bar, cinema, restaurant and record shop.
✉ 47 rue du Docteur-Fanton ☎ 04 90 49 56 77 🕐 daily 10–9 except Mon (2–9) & Thu (10–7)

Les Baux
Le Mas des Chevaliers
Traditional Provençal furniture and objets d'art.
✉ Vallon de la Fontaine ☎ 04 90 54 44 48

Alpes-Maritimes

Nice
Atelier Galerie Dury
Contemporary paintings, sculptures and reliefs of a nautical theme by award-winning artist Christian Dury.
✉ 31 rue Droite, Vieux-Nice ☎ 04 93 62 50 57 🚌 all buses

Galerie Ferrero
Exponents of the Nice School – very modern and very expensive.
✉ 24 rue de France/4 rue du Congrés ☎ 04 93 87 41 50/04 93 16 10 15

Specialist Shops

Vaucluse

Avignon
Papiers-Plumes
Beautiful pens, paper and desk objects for lovers of the art of letter writing.
✉ **45 rue Joseph Vernet** ☎ **04 90 82 68 77**

Scenes Interieures
A beautiful yet affordable rustic interior design and gift shop.
✉ **41 rue d'Amphoux** ☎ **04 90 86 46 31**

Bouches-du-Rhône

Aix
Cine-Photo Provence
Photographic equipment, films and a quality development service.
✉ **rue Bédarrides 20** ☎ **04 42 93 47 30**

Arles
Marie Coquine
Dolls, bears, hobby horses and clothes for tiny tots.
✉ **rue de l'Hôtel de Ville** ☎ **04 90 93 44 20**

Marseille
Centre Bourse
A vast indoor shopping mall containing Solaris (sunglasses), Yves Rocher (natural cosmetics), Habitat (interior design) and countless other specialist boutiques.
✉ **rue de Bir-Hakeim** 🚌 **Bus 31, 33, 34, 41, 80, 81**

Var and Haute-Provence

Briançon
Escale Location
Mountain sports kit from canoe-paddles to crampons.
✉ **avenue Vauban** ☎ **04 92 20 52 20**

Alpes-Maritimes

Antibes
Antibes Shipservices
Here you will find everything from 'boaty' keyrings to fashionable yachting gear.
✉ **31 rue Thuret** ☎ **04 93 34 75 96**

Cannes
Geneviève Lethu
A delightful gift shop, crammed from floor to ceiling with original presents and home decorations.
✉ **6 rue Maréchal Joffre** ☎ **04 93 68 18 19**

Mélonie
The most exquisite dried flower arrangements you are ever likely to see.
✉ **80 rue d'Antibes** ☎ **04 93 68 60 60**

Nice
Domaine Massa
Hidden in the steep, sun-soaked hills behind Nice, this old farm cultivates two distinctly *Niçois* products – carnations and *vin de Bellet* (see panel).
✉ **425 chemin de Crémat, 06200 Nice** ☎ **04 93 37 80 02**

Halogene
Trendy interior design store. Furniture, lighting and gift ideas.
✉ **21/23 rue de la Buffa** ☎ **04 93 88 96 26**

St Paul de Vence
Le Coucou
The witty hand-made ceramics here make highly original presents.
✉ **place de l'Église** ☎ **04 93 32 91 18**

A Little-Known Wine
Few people know about the tiny AOC wine region of Bellet near Nice, largely because the majority of the 160,000 or so bottles produced each year never gets any further than the cellars of the Riviera's top restaurants. The full-bodied red, with its wild cherry bouquet, can be aged up to 30 years. The golden white wine is reminiscent of *Chablis* and locals swear the rosé is the best accompaniment to regional fish dishes. Phone in advance for a tasting.

Amusement Parks, Sports & Museums

Snow Fun
Many of Provence's larger ski resorts offer excellent facilities for families with children of all ages, and a variety of winter sporting activities: ice skating, husky-mushing, tobogganing, horse-drawn sleigh rides. The family resort of Orcière-Merlettes has a crêche for children from nine months to six years, special Jardin des Neiges snow-fun kindergarten for children aged three and above, and children's skiing lessons. Serre Chevalier and Isola 2000 (➤ 115) offer similar facilities.

Bouches-du-Rhône
Aqualand
Children are happy to splash away countless hours in this aquatic paradise of pools and water games.
✉ 13240 Septemes-les-Vallons (off autoroute Aix-Marseille), Marseille ☎ 04 67 26 71 09 🕐 Jun to mid-Sept, 10–7

El Dorado City
A Wild West Park with pony rides, shows and entertainment in the middle of the Provence garrigue. Good fun for adults as well as children.
✉ 123320 Châteauneuf-les-Martigues ☎ 04 42 79 86 90 🕐 mid-Mar–end May, Wed, Sat, Sun & hols

Massalia Théâtre
Language proves no barrier when children's favourite fairytales come alive here (➤ 114).
✉ 41 rue Jobin, 3e, Marseille ☎ 04 91 11 45 65 🚌 bus 49A, 49B

La Petite Provence
A miniature Provençal village showing daily scenes at school, the market and in the café.
✉ avenue de la Vallée des Baux, Paradou ☎ 04 90 54 35 75 🕐 Jun–Sep, 10–7; Oct–May, 2–7

Parc Zoologique la Barben
Modern zoo with spacious enclosures for elephants, giraffes, tigers and white rhinos. Picnic area and playground.
✉ Route D572, between Salon-de Provence and Aix-en-Provence ☎ 04 90 55 19 12 🕐 10–6

Var and Haute-Provence
Aqualibre
Children's courses in Kayaking and white-water rafting in a safe environment. Polyglot instructors . Children must be able to swim.
✉ base Eau-Vive du Rioclar, 04340 Meolans-Revel ☎ 04 92 81 90 96 🕐 Course consists of five hour-long lessons

Orcières-Merlette Ski Resort
Family fun in the snow (➤ panel).
✉ Orcières-Merlette ☎ 04 92 55 89 89 (Tourist Office)

Port Grimaud Luna Park
Some of the most exhilarating fairground rides in Europe.
✉ Golfe de St Tropez ☎ 04 94 56 35 64 🕐 early Apr–late Jun, 8:30PM–1AM; late Jun–mid-Sep, 8:30PM–2AM; Sun & hols from 4PM

Village des Tortues
Children find the one-hour tour of this remarkable 'village' with its 1,200 turtles and tortoises, truly fascinating.
✉ 83590 Gonfaron (off autoroute Aix-Cannes) ☎ 04 94 78 26 41 🕐 Mar–Nov, daily 9AM–7PM

Alpes-Maritimes
Antibes Land
All ages enjoy this amusement park – its big wheel, roller coaster and even its bungee jumping!
✉ Route N7 (opposite Marineland), Antibes ☎ 04 93 95 23 03 🕐 Jun, 8PM–2AM; Jul–Aug, 3:30–2AM; Easter, Wed, Sat, Sun, hols, 2–2

Fun Kart
Go-karting for children and adults, just outside Grasse.
✉ Bar-sur-Loup (Route de Gourdon) ☎ 04 93 42 48 08
🕐 daily 12–6; Jul–Aug, 12–midnight

Grottes de St Cézaire
Fairytale world of rich red caves filled with 'musical' stalactites and stalagmites in magical shapes.
✉ St-Cézaire-sur-Siagne
☎ 04 93 60 22 35
🕐 Jun–Sep, 10:30–12, 2:30–6; Jul–Aug, 10:30–6:30; winter 2:30–5. Closed Nov–mid-Feb

Hippodrome
Spend a memorable family night out at the horse races.
✉ Hippodrome Cagnes, Cagnes-sur-Mer ☎ 04 93 22 51 00 🕐 early Jul–end Aug, Mon, Wed, Fri from 8:30PM

Kindia Park
A fun-park appealing to all ages with activities ranging from bouncy castles for tots to paint balls for teenagers.
✉ Parc Vaugrenier, Villeneuve-Loubet ☎ 04 93 65 61 92

Marineland
The greatest marine show in Europe (► panel).
✉ Route N7 (opposite Antibes Land), Antibes ☎ 04 93 33 49 49 🕐 daily 10–6

Musée National
A huge collection of dolls dating from the 18th century to Barbie.
✉ 17 avenue Princesse Grace, Monaco ☎ 04 93 30 91 26 🕐 Oct–Easter, 10–12:15, 2:30–6:30; Easter–Sep, 10–6:30. Closed 1 Jan, 1 May, 19 Nov, 25 Dec

Musée Oceanographique
Jacques Cousteau's world famous aquarium and marine museum appeals to children of all ages (► 83).
✉ avenue Saint-Martin, Monaco ☎ 04 90 15 36 00
🕐 Oct–Mar, 9.30–7; Apr–Jun & Sep, 9–7; Jul–Aug 9–8; Nov–Feb 10–6

Musée des Trains Miniatures
A fascinating railway museum.
✉ avenue Impératrice Eugénie, Nice ☎ 04 93 97 41 40
🕐 winter, 9:30–5; summer, 9:30–7 🚌 bus 22

Parc des Miniatures
More than 200 small-scale models tracing the vivid history of the French Riviera.
✉ Blvd Impératrice Eugénie, Nice ☎ 04 93 44 67 74
🕐 9AM–dusk 🚌 bus 22

Les Terrassas de Fontvieille
Prince Rainier's impressive collections of model boats and vintage cars, a zoo – and even a Macdonalds! Something for all members of the family in Monaco.
✉ Terraces de Fontfieille, Monaco ☎ zoo 04 93 25 18 31; naval museum 04 92 05 28 48; classic car exhibition 04 92 05 28 56 🕐 telephone for details

Visiobulle
Discover the underwater world of 'Millionaire's Bay' in a glass-bottomed boat. Reserve to avoid disappointment.
✉ Embarcadère Courbet, Juan-les-Pins ☎ 04 93 67 02 11
🕐 Apr–Sep, departures at 11, 1:30, 3, 4:30; also 9:30, 6 & evenings mid-Jun–Aug

Marineland
A wonderful world of performing sea-lions, killer whales, dolphins, and close underwater encounters with sharks (safely, within a transparent tunnel!). Children love the 'Jungle des Papillons' with exotic butterflies, huge, hairy spiders and other creepy-crawlies. Younger children enjoy the pony tours, face-painting and stroking the animals at 'La Petite Ferme Provençale'. Older children hurtle down the Aqua-Splash water slides and Mum and Dad try their hand at wacky crazy-golf. All this and more at Marineland.

Casinos, Cinemas & Nightspots

The Man Who Broke the Bank!
The glitz and glamour of the Riviera's casinos are famous the world-over, in particular the one at Monte Carlo (➤ 82) where Charles Deville Wells turned $400 into $40,000 in a 3-day gambling spree, thereby inspiring the song *The Man who Broke the Bank at Monte-Carlo*.

Vaucluse

Avignon
Koala Bar
This lively bar attracts a young international crowd.
✉ **2 place des Corps Saints**
☎ **04 90 86 80 87**
🕐 **weekdays 8:30AM–1AM, Sat 11:00–1, Sun 4PM–1.**

Peniche Dolphin Blues
A café-theatre on a barge moored on the Rhône near Avignon's famous bridge. Cabaret and live music most evenings and a children's theatre during the day.
✉ **Chemin de l'Île Piot** ☎ **04 90 82 46 96**

Utopia/Ajmi
Five film screens showing original version films, attached to the Ajmi Jazz Club. Dance spectacles and cabaret too.
✉ **4 rue Escalier Sainte-Anne**
☎ **04 90 82 65 36 (Ajmi 04 90 86 08 61)** 🕐 **Films most days (phone for details). Jazz nights: Thu & Fri**

Bouches-du-Rhône

Aix-en-Provence
Honky Tonk Pub
Dark, loud and smoky but currently very *in*. The DJ plays a mix of rock, disco, techno and funk.
✉ **38 rue de la Verrerie** ☎ **04 42 27 21 82** 🕐 **Tue–Sat, 7PM–2AM**

Mistral
Join the locals for the latest sounds in acid, techno, house and garage music. Overflowingly popular nightclub.
✉ **3 rue Fréderic Mistral**

☎ **04 42 38 16 49** 🕐 **Phone**

Scat Club
A traditional club with live jazz, soul, rhythm & blues, and reggae.
✉ **11 rue de la Verrerie** ☎ **04 42 23 00 23** 🕐 **Tue–Sat from 10:30PM**

Arles
La Café la Nuit
Popular meeting place at the heart of Arles and subject of a famous Van Gogh painting.
✉ **11 place du Forum** ☎ **04 90 96 44 56**

Aubagne
Espace 'Le Belle Epoque'
Atmospheric bar-cum-café theatre with live music, cabaret and readings.
✉ **4 Cours Foch** ☎ **04 42 03 13 66**

Marseille
Le Montana Blues
Live R&B, jazz and country at weekends.
✉ **2 rue Poggioli** ☎ **04 91 92 33 10** 🕐 **Open 11AM–5AM. Closed Sun** 🚌 **Bus 31, 33, 34, 41, 80, 81**

Trolleybus
Marseille's number one rock venue. Three bars and two bowling alleys.
✉ **24 quai Rive-Neuve** ☎ **04 91 54 30 45** 🕐 **Tue–Sat 11PM–5 or 6AM; Tue–Wed (bar only) open until 1 midnight.** 🚇 **Metro 1 (Vieux Port)**

Saintes-Maries-de-la-Mer
Bar-le Commerce
Café with live entertainment and frequent flamenco shows.
✉ **13 rue Victor Hugo** ☎ **04 90 97 84 11**

Var and Haute-Provence

St Tropez
Les Caves du Roy
St Tropez' spiciest nightspot.
✉ Hôtel Byblos, avenue Paul Signac ☎ 04 94 56 68 00
🕐 Easter–Oct 11PM–around 6AM

Alpes-Maritimes

Antibes
La Siesta
One of the Côte d'Azur's most exotic nightclubs with open-air dance floors, fountains, flaming torches and a wave-shaped casino.
✉ route du Bord-de-la-Mer (between Antibes and La Brague) ☎ 04 93 33 04 63
🕐 Open mid-May–mid-Sep 11PM–around 4AM

Monaco
Café de Paris
Even if you are not a big-spender, you will be tempted by the dazzling array of slot-machines in this famous café (see panel).
✉ place du Casino ☎ 04 92 16 20 20 🕐 all day from 10AM.

Le Casino
The most famous, ritziest casino on the Riviera, but with a F50 entrance fee.
✉ place du Casino ☎ 04 92 16 21 21 🕐 From 3PM till dawn

Cinema d'Été
An open-air cinema, summertime only.
✉ Avenue Princesse Grace
☎ 04 93 25 86 80

Monte Carlo
Jimmi'z
Wear your finery to join the jet set at the chicest disco on the Riviera.
✉ 26 avenue Princesse Grace

☎ 04 93 16 22 77
🕐 11.30PM–around 5AM

Nice
Casino Ruhl
Nice's glitzy, glamorous casino offers spectacular dinner cabarets as well as private gaming rooms.
✉ Promenade des Anglais
☎ 04 93 87 95 87

Cinémathèque
Golden oldies in original version as well as the latest releases.
✉ 3 Esplanade Kennedy
☎ 04 92 04 06 66 🕐 Tel for details 🚌 all buses

La Douche
This tiny, crowded nightclub also contains France's first cyber-café.
✉ 34 cours Saleya ☎ 04 93 92 34 34 🕐 11AM–2:30AM
🚌 all buses

Le Duke
Intimate bar for night owls, with a small dance floor, predominantly black music and plenty of ambiance.
✉ 11 rue Alexandre Mari
☎ 04 93 62 61 96 🕐 1AM–5AM
🚌 all buses

L'Iguane
An old-established Niçois nightspot on the old port, with tropical guerrilla decor.
✉ 5 quai des deux Emmanuel
☎ 04 93 56 83 83 🕐 Open 7 days a week 🚌 Bus 2, 9, 10

Le Salon
A trendy after-dinner venue with sumptuous theatrical baroque décor, cocktail evenings and fancy-dress theme nights.
✉ 2 rue Bréa ☎ 04 93 92 92 91 🕐 Mon–Sat from 10:30PM–2:30AM. 🚌 all buses

Café de Paris
This beautifully renovated Art Deco triumph contains a restaurant as well as a gaming house, which in its heyday attracted the world's most élite society. Ladies' man Edward VII was a frequent visitor, and the delicious dessert crêpe suzette was created here, named after one of his companions.

113

Theatre, Opera, Classical Music

Nice's Acropolis
Love it or hate it, one thing is for sure – you can't ignore this monstrous mass of smoked glass and concrete slabs at the very hub of modern Nice. Nevertheless, with its four high-tech auditoria, concert hall, bowling alley, exhibition halls, cinémathèque (▶ 114) and extensive conference facilities, it has been voted 'Europe's best congress centre' for the past three years.

Ticket Sales

Avignon
Fnac
✉ 19 rue de la République
☎ 04 90 14 35 35

Marseille
✉ Centre Commercial Borse
☎ 04 91 39 94 00

Virgin Megastore
✉ 75 rue St-Ferréol ☎ 04 91 55 55 00

Nice
✉ C30 avenue Jean Médecin
☎ 04 91 55 55 00

Vaucluse

Avignon
L'opéra
Frequent concerts by the local *Orchestra Lyrique de Région Avignon-Provence*. Also ballet and opera.
✉ place de l'Horloge ☎ 04 90 82 23 44

Théâtre du Chêne Noir
Small theatre with a first class repertory company.
✉ 8 bis rue Ste-Catherine
☎ 04 90 82 40 57

Orange
Théâtre Antique
Concerts, opera and theatre spectaclar in an exceptional setting (▶ 26).
✉ Place des Frères-Mounet
☎ 04 90 51 17 10

Bouches-du-Rhône

Aix
Théâtre duJeu de Paume
Aix's number one theatre and concert venue.
✉ 17–21 rue de l'Opera ☎ 04 42 38 44 71

Marseille
Massalia Théâtre
France's first marionnette theatre (▶ 110).
✉ 41 rue Jobin, 3e ☎ 04 91 11 45 65 🚌 bus 49A,49B

L'opéra de Marseille
Predominantly Italian opera. Roland Petit's famous National Ballet Company is also based here.
✉ place Reyer ☎ 04 91 55 00 70 🚇 Metro 1 (Vieux Port)

Theatre National de Marseille la Criée
Marseille's leading theatre, housed in a former fish auction house, giving widely acclaimed performances.
✉ 30 rue de Rive-Neuve, 7e
☎ 04 91 54 70 54 🚌 Bus 31,33,34,41,80,81

Alpes-Maritimes

Nice
L'Acropolis
This vast, modern congress, arts and tourism centre is popular for theatre, films and concerts (▶ panel).
✉ 1 Esplanade Kennedy
☎ 04 93 92 83 00 🚌 all buses

Opéra de Nice
Home of the Nice Opera, the Philharmonic Orchestra and Ballet Corps, a rococo extravaganza in red and gold modelled on the Naples Opera House.
✉ 4/6 rue Saint François de Paule ☎ 04 92 17 40 40 🚌 all buses

Théâtre de Nice (TDN)
This modern theatre presents world-class shows.
✉ promenade des Arts ☎ 04 93 80 52 60 🚌 all buses

Participatory Sports

Alpine skiing

Isola 2000
Day trips from Nice coach station include a ski pass.
☎ 04 93 23 15 15

Serre Chevalier
Provence's premier ski resort, near Briançon.
☎ 04 92 21 08 50

Ballooning

Ulysse Aventure
The ultimate way to explore Provence.
✉ BP No 17, 13570 Barbentane
☎ 04 90 95 53 28

Canoeing

Kayak Vert, Fontaine-de-Vaucluse
The scenic river Sorgue is a favourite venue for canoeing and kayaking enthusiasts.
✉ 84800 Fontaine-de-Vaucluse
☎ 04 90 20 35 44

Cross-Country Skiing

Gap Bayard
One of the largest ski de fond regions in the Hautes Alpes.
☎ 04 92 50 16 83

Deep-sea Fishing

Guiguot Marine, Antibes
Tired of lazing on the beach? Book a day trip out at sea.
✉ avenue 11 Novembre ☎ 04 93 34 17 17 🕐 Jun–Oct

Golf

Royal Mougins Golf Club
Considered by many the best golf club on the Côte d'Azur.
✉ 424 avenue du Roi ☎ 04 92 92 49 69

Hang-Gliding

The most popular areas are Mont Ventoux and the Lubéron.
✉ Association Vaucluse Parapente, 26 rue des Teinturiers, Avignon ☎ 04 90 85 67 82

River Cruises

Mireio, Avignon
Explore the Provençal waterways.
✉ allée de l'Oulle ☎ 04 90 85 62 25

Sailing

Centre Nautique Municipal, Cannes
Hire and tuition in sailing dinghies, catamarans and windsurfing for adults and children.
✉ 9 rue Esprit Violet ☎ 04 92 18 88 88

Scuba Diving

Comité Régional des Sports Sous-Marins, Marseille
The Riviera offers some of the finest diving in Europe.
✉ 24 quai de Rive-Neuve
🕐 04 91 09 36 31

Tennis

LawnTennis Club Suzanne Lenguen, Nice
Venue of the Nice Open and former club of French tennis star, Yannick Noah.
✉ 5 av Suzanne Lenguen
☎ 04 93 96 17 70

Yacht Charter

Moorings, Nice
Skippered yacht, for hire.
✉ quai Amiral Infernet ☎ 04 92 00 42 22

Spectator Sports

The region's number one spectator sport is le foot (football) and its top team, Olympique de Marseille, (☎ 04 91 76 56 09 for tickets). In the Camargue area, the most popular sport is bullfighting (see page 50) but the Monte Carlo Rally (Jan) and Monaco's Formula One Grand Prix (May) and the Monte Carlo and Nice Open Tennis Championships (April) are also huge crowd-pullers, along with regular horse-racing at Cagnes and Marseilles.

All France is fanatical about cycling, with the Tour de France scaling some of Provence's highest mountain passes. Also every summer, crowds flock to Nice for its international triathlon (cycling, running, swimming) – the so-called 'Madman's Promenade'.

What's On When

Christmas Mass
Provençal midnight mass takes place at Aix, Les Baux, Fontvieille, St-Rémy, Séguret, Tarascon

January
Monte Carlo Car Rally (end of month, ► 115)

February
Nice Carnival (2 weeks, ► 60–1)
Monte Carlo International Circus Festival
Fête du Citron, Menton (10 days at Carnival, ► 60–1)
Corso du Mimosa, Bormes-les-Mimosas (10 Feb, ► 60)

March
Dance Festival, Cannes

April
International Tennis Open, Nice and Monaco
Ski Grand Prix, Isola 2000
Winegrowers' Festival, Châteauneuf-du-Pape (25 Apr)
Easter Festival and start of bullfighting season, Arles (4 days at Easter)
Fête des Gardians, Arles (last Sunday, ► 60)

May
Cannes Film Festival (2nd week, ► 85, 60)
Fête de la Rose, Grasse (2nd weekend)
Bravade de St-Torpes, St Tropez (16–17 May, ► 66)
Formula One Grand Prix, Monaco; Ochre Festival, Roussillon(Ascension weekend)
Gypsy Pilgrimage, Saintes-Maries-de-la-Mer (24–25 May, ► 57)

June
Dance, music and folklore Festival, Arles
Jazz Festival, Aix
Sacred Music Festival, Nice
Fête de la Tarasque, Tarascon (last Sun, ► 58)

July
Nice Jazz Festival (first 2 weeks)

International Folklore Festival, Marseille (first 2 weeks)
Rencontres Internationales de la Photographie, Arles
International Music Festival, Aix (last 3 weeks, ► 60)
Annual Provençal Boules Competition, Marseille (mid-Jul, ► 60)
Chorègies Music Festival, Orange (last 2 weeks)
Food Festival, Carpentras (3rd weekend)
International Art Festival, Cagnes
International Theatre Festival, Avignon (mid Jul– mid Aug, ► 60)
International Fireworks Festival, Monaco (Jul–Aug, ► 60)
Numerous Arts festivals at Arles, Gordes, Fontaine-de-Vaucluse, Menton, Sisteron, St-Paul-de-Vence, Vaison-la-Romaine, Vence and other towns and villages (Jul/Aug)

August
Grape-ripening Festival, Châteauneuf-du-Pape (1st weekend, ► 60)
Lavender Festival, Digne (► 60)
Fête de St-Laurent, Eygalières (9–11 Aug, ► 56)

September
Rice Harvest Festival and end of bullfighting season, Arles (2nd Sun)
Nioulargue Yacht Regatta, St Tropez (End Sep–1st week Oct)

October
International Folklore Fair, Marseille

November
Truffle Fair, Carpentras (last Fri)
Santon Fair, Marseille (last Sun–Epiphany)

Practical Matters

TIME DIFFERENCES

GMT
12 noon

France
1PM

→
Germany
1PM

←
USA (NY)
7AM

→
Netherlands
1PM

→
Spain
1PM

BEFORE YOU GO

WHAT YOU NEED

● Required
○ Suggested
▲ Not required

	UK	Germany	USA	Netherlands	Spain
Passport/National Identity Card	●	●	●	●	●
Visa	▲	▲	▲	▲	▲
Onward or Return Ticket	▲	▲	▲	▲	▲
Health Inoculations	▲	▲	▲	▲	▲
Health Documentation (reciprocal agreement document) (➤ 123, Health)	●	●	▲	●	●
Travel Insurance	○	○	○	○	○
Driving Licence (national)	●	●	●	●	●
Car Insurance Certificate (if own car)	○	○	○	○	○
Car Registration Document (if own car)	●	●	●	●	●

WHEN TO GO

Provence/Côte d'Azur

High season

Low season

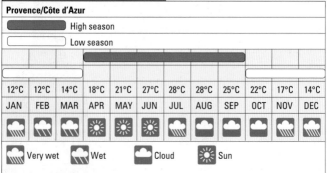

12°C	12°C	14°C	18°C	21°C	27°C	28°C	28°C	25°C	22°C	17°C	14°C
JAN	FEB	MAR	APR	MAY	JUN	JUL	AUG	SEP	OCT	NOV	DEC

Very wet   Wet   Cloud   Sun

TOURIST OFFICES

In the UK
French Tourist
Office
178 Piccadilly
London W1V 0AL
☎ 0891 244123
(recorded infor-
mation)

Monaco
Government
Tourist and
Convention Office
3–18 Chelsea
Garden Market
London SW10 0XE
☎ 0500 006114

In the USA
French
Government
Tourist Office
444 Madison
Avenue, 16th floor
New York. NY10022
☎ 212/838 7800

Monaco
Government
Tourist and
Convention Bureau
565 Fifth Avenue,
23rd floor, New
York NY10017
☎ 800/753 9696

POLICE 17

FIRE 18

AMBULANCE 15

SOS TRAVELLERS 04 91 62 12 80

WHEN YOU ARE THERE

ARRIVING

The national airline, Air France (☎ 0802 802 802 in France). has scheduled flights from Britain, mainland Europe and beyond, to Marseille and Nice. French Railways (SNCF) operate high speed trains (TGV) from Paris to main Provence and Côte d'Azur stations.

Marseille-Provence Airport Journey times
Kilometres to city centre

25 kilometres	🚇	N/A
	🚍	25 minutes
	🚗	30 minutes

Nice-Côte d'Azur Airport Journey times
Kilometres to city centre

7 kilometres	🚇	N/A
	🚍	20 minutes
	🚗	15 minutes

MONEY

The monetary unit of France and Monaco is the French franc (FF) which is divided into 100 centimes.

There are coins of 5, 10, 20, and 50 centimes, and 1, 2, 5, 10 and 20 francs.
Notes are issued in 20, 50, 100, 200 and 500 francs.

Monaco has its own coins of the same value as French coins also in circulation, but they are not generally accepted outside the Principality.

TIME

 France is one hour ahead of Greenwich Mean Time (GMT+1), but from late March, when clocks are put forward one hour, until late October, French summer time (GMT +2) operates.

CUSTOMS

 YES

Goods Obtained Duty Free Inside the EU or Goods Bought Outside the EU (Limits):
Alcohol (over 22° vol): 1L *or*
Alcohol (not over 22° vol): 2L *and* Still table wine: 2L
Cigarettes: 200 *or*
Cigars: 50 *or*
Tobacco: 250gms
Perfume: 60ml
Toilet water: 250ml
Goods Bought Duty and Tax Paid Inside the EU (Guidance Levels):
Alcohol (over 22° vol): 10L
Alcohol (not over 22° vol): 20L
Wine (max 60L sparkling): 90L
Beer: 110L
Cigarettes: 800 *or*
Cigars: 200 *or*
Tobacco: 1kg
Perfume: no limit
Toilet Water: no limit
You must be 17 and over to benefit from the alcohol and tobacco allowances.

 NO

Drugs, firearms, ammunition, offensive weapons, obscene material, unlicensed animals.

CONSULATES

UK	**Germany**	**USA**	**Netherlands**	**Spain**
04 91 15 72 10 (Mar)	04 91 16 75 20 (Mar)	04 91 54 92 00 (Mar)	04 91 25 66 64 (Mar)	04 91 00 32 70 (Mar)
04 93 82 32 04 (N)	04 93 83 55 25 (N)	04 93 88 89 55 (N)	04 91 87 52 94 (N)	93 30 24 98 (N)
(377) 93 50 99 66 (M)	(377) 93 30 19 49 (M)		(377) 92 05 15 02 (M)	(377) 93 30 24 98 (M)

Key: (Mar) - Marseille (N) - Nice (M) - Monaco

WHEN YOU ARE THERE

TOURIST OFFICES

Provence and Côte d'Azur
● Comité Régional de
Tourisme Provence-Alpes-
Côte d'Azur
Espace Colbert

14 rue Sainte-Barbe
13231 Marseille Cedex 01
☎ 04 91 39 38 00
Fax: 04 91 56 66 61

Department Offices
● Comité Régional de
Tourisme Riviéra Côte
d'Azur
55 promenade des Anglais
BP 602, 06011 Nice
☎ 04 93 37 78 78
Fax: 04 93 86 01 06

● Comité Départemental de
Tourisme des Bouches-
du-Rhône
Le Montesquieu
13 rue Roux de Brignoles
13006 Marseille
☎ 04 91 13 84 13
Fax: 04 91 33 01 82

● Comité Départemental du
Tourisme du Vaucluse
2 rue St Etienne
BP 147, 84008 Avignon
☎ 04 90 86 43 42
Fax: 04 90 86 54 77

Monaco
● Direction du Tourisme et
des Congrès de la
Principauté de Monaco
2A boulevard des Moulins
Monte-Carlo
MC 98030 Monaco Cedex
☎ (377) 92 16 61 66
Fax: (377) 92 16 60 00
Look for 🛈 for information
in other towns and villages.

NATIONAL HOLIDAYS

J	F	M	A	M	J	J	A	S	O	N	D
2		(2)	(2)	3(4)	1(2)	1	1			3	2

1 Jan	New Year's Day
27 Jan	St Devote's Day (Monaco only)
Mar/Apr	Easter Sunday and Monday
1 May	Labour Day
8 May	VE Day (France only)
May/Jun	Whit Sunday and Monday
June	Corpus Christi (Monaco only)
14 July	Bastille Day (France only)
15 Aug	Assumption
1 Nov	All Saints' Day
11 Nov	Remembrance Day (France only)
19 Nov	Monaco National Holiday (Monaco only)
9 Dec	Immaculate Conception (Monaco only)
25 Dec	Christmas Day

OPENING HOURS

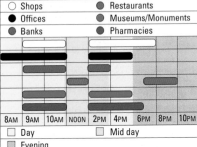

○ Shops	● Restaurants
● Offices	● Museums/Monuments
● Banks	● Pharmacies

| □ Day | ▨ Mid day |
| ▨ Evening | |

In addition to the times shown above, afternoon time
of shops in summer is 4 to 8 or 9PM. Most shops close
Sunday and many on Monday. Small food shops open
from 7AM and may open Sunday morning. Large
department stores do not close for lunch and hyper-
markets open 10AM to 9 or 10PM but may shut Monday
morning. Banks are closed Sunday as well as
Saturday or Monday.

Museums and monuments have extended summer
hours. Many close one day a week; either Monday
(municipal ones) or Tuesday (national ones).

DRIVE ON THE RIGHT

TOILETS CHARGE

PUBLIC TRANSPORT

Internal Flights Air Inter – information via Air France (▶ 119, **Arriving**) and travel agents – is the French internal airline, linking 45 cities and towns, among them Marseille, Toulon, Avignon, Nîmes, Nice, Cannes and Fréjus. Some private airlines serve smaller towns.

Trains The main line in Provence and the Côte d'Azur links the towns and cities of the coast with the Rhône Valley, with Marseille as its hub. A spectacular stretch runs behind the coast from Fréjus/St Raphaël to Menton, which in summer is the most efficient way to move along the coast.

Area Buses Services run by a number of private companies are punctual and comfortable, but not very frequent outside main urban areas and coastal resorts. There are also SNCF buses which serve places on rail routes where trains do not stop. Bus stations: Marseille (☎ 04 91 08 16 40), Nice (☎ 04 93 85 61 81)

Island Ferries There are ferries to the three islands off the coast of Hyères (the Iles d'Hyères (Porquerolles, Port-Cros, and Ile de Levant) from five ports along the Côte d'Azur (Cavalaire, Le Lavandou, Port d'Hyères, Toulon and La Tour Fondue). Some services operate summer only.

Urban Transport Most sizeable towns have a bus station (*gare routière*), often near the railway station. Services, even in cities, stop about 9PM. The most efficient bus network is in Nice, where computerised signboards at every bus-stop inform you of the exact time of arrival of your service.

CAR RENTAL

All the main car-rental companies have desks at Marseille and Nice airports and in main towns. Car hire is expensive, but airlines and tour operators offer fly-drive, and French Railways (SNCF) train/car packages, often more economical than hiring locally.

TAXIS

Taxis are very expensive and not allowed to cruise. They must pick up at ranks (*stations de taxi*) found at airports, railway stations and elsewhere. Always check there is a meter. There is a pick-up charge plus a rate per minute – check with the driver.

DRIVING

Speed limits on toll motorways: **130kph (110kph when wet)**; non-toll motorways and dual carriageways: **110kph (100kph when wet)**. In fog (visibility less than 50m): **50kph all roads**

Speed limits on country roads: **90kph (80kph when wet)**

Speed limits on urban roads: **50kph** (limit starts at town sign)

Must be worn in front seats at all times and in rear seats where fitted.

Random breath-testing is frequent. Limit: 0.05 per cent alcohol per litre of blood.

Petrol (*essence*) including unleaded (*sans plomb*) is widely available. Petrol stations are numerous along main roads but rarer in mountainous areas. Some on minor roads are closed on Sundays. Maps showing petrol stations are available from main tourist offices.

A red warning triangle must be carried if your car has no hazard warning lights, but it is advised for all motorists. Place this 30m behind the car in the event of an accident or breakdown. On motorways ring from emergency phones (every 2km) to contact the breakdown service. Off motorways, police will advise on local breakdown services.

At the top is a ruler scale:

CENTIMETRES 0 1 2 3 4 5 6 7 8

INCHES 0 1 2 3

PERSONAL SAFETY

The *Police Municipale* (blue uniforms) carry police duties in cities and towns. The *Gendarmes* (blue trousers, black jackets, white belts), the national police force, cover the countryside and smaller places. The *CRS* deal with emergencies and also look after safety on beaches. Monaco has its own police.

To avoid danger or theft:
- Do not use unmanned roadside rest areas at night.
- Cars, especially foreign cars, shoud be secured.
- In crowded places, beware of pickpockets.

Police assistance:
☎ **17**
from any call box

TELEPHONES

All telephone numbers in France comprise ten digits (eight in Monaco). There are no area codes except for Monaco (377 precedes number when phoning from outside the Principality). Coins required: 50 centimes, 1, 5 or 10 francs. Phone cards (*télécartes*) are sold in units of 50 or 120 in post offices, tobacconists and newagents.

International Dialling Codes

From France and Monaco to:	
UK:	00 44
Germany:	00 49
USA:	00 1
Netherlands:	00 31
Spain:	00 34

POST

Post Offices
The PTT (*Poste et Télécommunications*) deals with mail and telephone services. Outside main centres, post offices open shorter hours and may close 12–2. Letter boxes are yellow. Open: 8–7 (12 Sat). Closed: Sun
☎ 04 91 15 40 00 (Marseille)
☎ (377) 93 25 11 11 (Monaco)

ELECTRICITY

The native power supply is: 220 volts

Type of socket:
Round-two hole sockets taking two-round-pin (or occasionally three-round-pin plugs. British visitors should bring an adaptor; US visitors a voltage transformer.

TIPS/GRATUITIES

Yes ✓ No ✗		
Restaurants (service incl; tip optional)	✗	
Cafés (service included; tip optional)	✗	
Hotels (service included; tip optional)	✗	
Hairdressers	✓	(5/10F)
Taxis	✓	(5/10F)
Tour guides	✓	(5/10F)
Cinema usherettes	✓	(5/10F)
Porters	✓	(5/10F)
Cloakroom attendants	✓	(small)
Toilets	✓	(small)

PHOTOGRAPHY

What to photograph: From the snow-peaked lower Alps to the 'Grand' canyons of central Provence and the *calanques* (narrow coastal inlets). The bright Provence light further enhances the beauty of the landscape.
Where to buy film: The most popular brands and types of film can be bought from shops and photo laboratories. Film development is quite expensive.
Restrictions: Some museums will allow you to photograph inside. In churches with frescoes and icons, prior permission for flashlight is required.

HEALTH

Insurance
Nationals of EU countries can obtain medical treatment at reduced cost on production of a qualifying form (Form E111 for Britons); however this does not apply to Monaco. Private medical insurance is advisable for all.

Dental Services
As for general medical treatment (▶ above, **Insurance**), nationals of EU countries can obtain dental treatment at reduced cost. Around 70 per cent of dentists' standard fees are refunded. Private medical insurance is still advisable for all.

Sun Advice
The sunshine yearly average is 2,500 hours, rising to 3,000 hours along the coast. Summers, particularly July and August, are dry and hot. If walking, wear a hat and drink plenty of fluids. On the beach, a high-protection sunscreen is a must.

Drugs
Pharmacies – recognised by their green cross sign – possess highly qualified staff able to offer medical advice, provide first aid and prescribe and provide a wide range of drugs, though some are available by prescription (*ordonnance*) only.

Safe Water
It is safe to drink tap water served in hotels and restaurants, but never drink from a tap marked *eau non potable*. Many prefer the taste of bottled water which is cheap and widely available.

CONCESSIONS

Students/Youths A youth card (*Carte Jeune*), available to those under 26, entitles holders to various discounts on public transport, museum admissions, entertainments, shopping and other facilities (including meals in university canteens): ask at tourist offices and post offices for details.

Senior Citizens A number of tour companies offer special arrangements for senior citizens; for further information contact the French Tourist Office (▶ 118, **Tourist Offices**). Senior citizens (aged over 60) are eligible for reduced or free entrance to sights, and (aged over 65) are eligible for fare discounts on public transport.

CLOTHING SIZES

France	UK	Rest of Europe	USA	
46	36	46	36	Suits
48	38	48	38	
50	40	50	40	
52	42	52	42	
54	44	54	44	
56	46	56	46	
41	7	41	8	Shoes
42	7.5	42	8.5	
43	8.5	43	9.5	
44	9.5	44	10.5	
45	10.5	45	11.5	
46	11	46	12	
37	14.5	37	14.5	Shirts
38	15	38	15	
39/40	15.5	39/40	15.5	
41	16	41	16	
42	16.5	42	16.5	
43	17	43	17	
36	8	34	6	Dresses
38	10	36	8	
40	12	38	10	
42	14	40	12	
44	16	42	14	
46	18	44	16	
38	4.5	38	6	Shoes
38	5	38	6.5	
39	5.5	39	7	
39	6	39	7.5	
40	6.5	40	8	
41	7	41	8.5	

- Contact the airport or airline on the day prior to leaving to ensure that the flight details are unchanged.
- There is an airport departure tax of 22F for international flights and 15F for internal flights.
- Check the duty-free limits of the country you are entering before departure.

LANGUAGE

French is the native language. In Monaco the traditional Monégasque language (a mixture of French, Provençal and Italian Ligurian) is spoken by the older generation. English is spoken by those involved in tourist trades and in the larger cosmopolitan centres – less so in smaller, rural places. However, attempts to speak French will always be appreciated. Below is a list of a few helpful words.
More extensive coverage can be found in the AA's *Essential French Phrase Book*.

hotel	l'hôtel	rate	le tarif
room	la chambre	breakfast	le petit déjeuner
single room	une personne	toilet	la toilette
double room	deux personnes	bathroom	le salle de bain
per person	par personne	shower	la douche
per room	par chambre	balcony	le balcon
one/two nights	une/deux nuits	key	la clef/clé
reservation	la réservation	chambermaid	femme de chambre

bank	la banque	American dollar	le dollar
exchange office	le bureau de change	banknote	le billet
		coin	la pièce
post office	la poste	credit card	la carte de crédit
cashier	le caissier	traveller's cheque	le chèque de voyage
foreign exchange	le change extérieur	exchange rate	le taux de change
English pound	la livre sterling	commission	la commission

restaurant	le restaurant	starter	le hors d'oeuvres
café	la café	main course	le plat principal
table	la table	dish of the day	le plat du jour
menu	le menu	dessert	le dessert
set menu	le menu du jour	drink	la boisson
wine list	la carte des vins	waiter	le garçon
lunch	le déjeuner	waitress	la serveuse
dinner	le dîner	the bill	l'addition

aeroplane	l'avion	ticket	le billet
airport	l'aéroport	single/return	simple/retour
train	le train	ticket office	le guichet
train station	la gare	timetable	l'horaire
bus	l'autobus	seat	la place
bus station	la gare routière	non smoking	non-fumeurs
ferry/boat	le bateau	reserved	réservée
port	le port	window	la fenêtre

yes	oui	tomorrow	demain
no	non	yesterday	hier
please	s'il vous-plaît	how much?	combien?
thank you	merci	expensive	cher
hello	bonjour	open	ouvert
goodbye	au revoir	closed	fermé
goodnight	bonsoir	second class	deuxième classe
sorry	pardon	first class	première classe
excuse me	excuse-moi	you're welcome	de rien/avec plaisir
help!	au secours!	okay	d'accord
today	aujourd'hui	I don't know	Je ne sais pas

INDEX

INDEX

Acknowledgements
The Automobile Association wishes to thank the following libraries, photographers and associations for their assistance in the preparation of this book.

THE BRIDGEMAN ART LIBRARY, LONDON 22 The Rocaille Armchair, 1946 by Henri Matisse (1869–1954) Musée Matisse, Nice-Cimiez
MARY EVANS PICTURE LIBRARY 11
THE RONALD GRANT ARCHIVE 86
ROBERT HARDING PICTURE LIBRARY 15a, 16, 21, 77
IMAGES COLOUR LIBRARY F/Cover: lavender field
MAGNUM PHOTOS LTD 14 (Eve Arnold)
M R I BANKERS' GUIDE TO FOREIGN CURRENCY 119
PICTURES COLOUR LIBRARY F/Cover: local man, 62, 85
SPECTRUM COLOUR LIBRARY 122b
WORLD PICTURES 1

The remaining pictures are from the Association's own library (**AA PHOTO LIBRARY**) with contributions from:
ADRIAN BAKER B/Cover: sunflowers, 9c, 15b, 18, 19, 20, 23, 24/5, 26, 27a, 31, 32, 33, 35, 38, 40, 41, 44, 46, 49, 55, 59, 61b, 63, 67, 71b, 76, 82, 87, 88, 91a; PAUL KENWARD 47; ROB MOORE 6, 79; ROGER MOSS 122a, 122c; TONY OLIVER F/Cover: folk dolls, 68; NEIL RAY 60, 117a; KEV REYNOLDS 13; BARRIE SMITH 27b, 28/9, 66, 71a, 73, 74; RICK STRANGE 2, 5a, 5b, 7, 8a, 8b, 9a, 9b, 12a, 12b, 17, 34, 36a, 36b, 37, 39, 42, 43, 45, 48, 50, 52, 57, 58, 61a, 64, 65, 78, 80, 81, 89, 90, 91b, 117b

Author's Acknowledgements
Teresa Fisher wishes to thank British Midland, National Express, Primotel Suiss, Hotel Solara, Nice, Hotel Martinez, Cannes, Mas de Chastelas, St Tropez, Hotel Calendal, Arles, the Tourist Offices of Nice, Arles and the Var and, in particular, Sylvie Gauchet.

Contributors
Copy editor: Penny Phenix   Page Layout: Design 23   Verifier: David Hancock
Researcher (Practical Matters): Colin Follett   Indexer: Marie Lorimer

Dear Essential Traveller

Your comments, opinions and recommendations are very important to us. So please help us to improve our travel guides by taking a few minutes to complete this simple questionnaire.

You do not need a stamp (unless posted outside the UK). If you do not want to cut this page from your guide, then photocopy it or write your answers on a plain sheet of paper.

Send to: **The Editor, AA World Travel Guides, FREEPOST SCE 4598, Basingstoke RG21 4GY.**

Your recommendations...

We always encourage readers' recommendations for restaurants, nightlife or shopping – if your recommendation is used in the next edition of the guide, we will send you a *FREE* AA *Essential* **Guide** of your choice. Please state below the establishment name, location and your reasons for recommending it.

_____

_____

_____

_____

Please send me **AA *Essential*** _____

(*see list of titles inside the front cover*)

About this guide...

Which title did you buy?

AA *Essential* _____

Where did you buy it? _____

When? m m / y y

Why did you choose an AA *Essential* Guide? _____

_____

_____

_____

_____

Did this guide meet your expectations?

Exceeded ☐ Met all ☐ Met most ☐ Fell below ☐

Please give your reasons _____

_____

_____

_____

continued on next page...

Were there any aspects of this guide that you particularly liked? _____

_____

_____

_____

Is there anything we could have done better? _____

_____

_____

_____

_____

About you...

Name (*Mr/Mrs/Ms*) _____

Address _____

_____

_____ Postcode _____

Daytime tel nos _____

Which age group are you in?
Under 25 ☐ 25–34 ☐ 35–44 ☐ 45–54 ☐ 55–64 ☐ 65+ ☐

How many trips do you make a year?
Less than one ☐ One ☐ Two ☐ Three or more ☐

Are you an AA member? Yes ☐ No ☐

About your trip...

When did you book? m m / y y   When did you travel? m m / y y
How long did you stay? _____
Was it for business or leisure? _____
Did you buy any other travel guides for your trip?
If yes, which ones? _____

_____

Thank you for taking the time to complete this questionnaire. Please send
it to us as soon as possible, and remember, you do not need a stamp
(*unless posted outside the UK*).

Happy Holidays!

The AA, its subsidiaries and any other companies or bodies in which it has an interest (the AA
Group) may use information about you to send you details of other products and services. The AA
Group as a matter of policy does not release its lists to third parties.
If you do not wish to receive further information please tick the box... ☐